THE FUGUE IN
BEETHOVEN'S PIANO MUSIC

STUDIES IN THE HISTORY OF MUSIC

EDITED BY EGON WELLESZ
C.B.E., F.B.A., Hon. D.Mus. Oxon.
Fellow of Lincoln College

Uniform with this Volume

MUSIC IN MEDIEVAL BRITAIN
by Frank Harrison

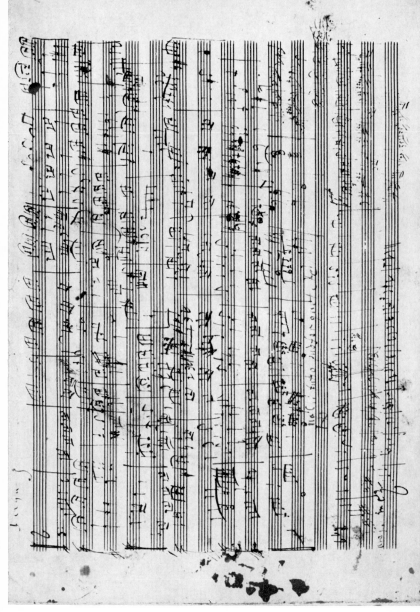

The only known fugue for keyboard by Beethoven that is both complete and not part of a larger work (see Chapter III). *British Museum Add. MS. 29801, fo. 158*

THE FUGUE IN
BEETHOVEN'S PIANO
MUSIC

by
JOHN V. COCKSHOOT

Routledge & Kegan Paul

LONDON

First published 1959
by Routledge & Kegan Paul Limited
Broadway House, Carter Lane, E.C.4
Printed in Great Britain
by Butler & Tanner Limited
Frome and London

TO MY WIFE
AND IN MEMORY OF
MY DEAREST PARENTS

CONTENTS

PLATE

The only known fugue for keyboard by Beethoven that is both complete and not part of a larger work (see Chapter. III).

British Museum Add. MS. 29801, fo. 158

Frontispiece

PREFACE

Beethoven's abilities as a writer of fugues are so generally discounted that this study is largely the result of a desire to trace what factors affected the manner of his fugal writing, with reference to his music for pianoforte solo, and to show by means of analysis the distinctive value of the fugues.

Analysis into Subjects, Answers, Expositions, Middle Sections, and so on, can give only a superficial idea of the workmanship that goes into making a fugue. The detailed critical and stylistic analyses of Beethoven's pianoforte fugues which follow try to achieve a clearer insight into the ways of his musical thought, and to lead to a better appreciation of his artistry and genius.

Beethoven's sketch-books naturally play an important part in any discussion of his music. Many attempts were made to trace the present whereabouts of the relevant sketches in the preparation of this study. They are mostly in German and Austrian libraries. The enquiries revealed that, in a number of cases, sketch-books had been moved to other libraries for safe keeping during the war of 1939–45, along with thousands of other books, which all awaited cataloguing. Those libraries which had escaped damage were more anxious to provide microfilms of their books to other less fortunate libraries, than to supply my needs, and this was understandable. The only really satisfactory solution to the problem was to visit the various libraries and inspect the original sketch-books at first hand. For various reasons this course was, unfortunately, not open to me.

Faced with these difficulties, I was reluctantly obliged to take this material at second hand. The obvious source of information about the sketches is in the publications of Gustav Nottebohm (1817–82). Nottebohm enjoys a great reputation for his two volumes of *Beethoveniana* and another devoted to Beethoven's

xi

studies. Evidently, Nottebohm examined all the available sketch-books. From his descriptions, these must have contained large numbers of sketches. Unfortunately, the volumes of *Beethoveniana* reproduce only a mere sample in comparison. One dearly wishes that Nottebohm had published all the sketches in full. Instead, one frequently finds sketches for only an opening theme, with no indication of how Beethoven wrought later sections of the work. In some cases, Heinrich Schenker, in his *Die letzten fünf Sonaten von Beethoven*, usually referred to as the *Erläuterungsausgabe*, quotes additional sketches, particularly with regard to the fugue in the Sonata in A flat, Op. 110. The study by Paul Mies, *Die Bedeutung der Skizzen Beethovens zur Erkenntnis seines Stiles*, insofar as it concerns the fugues, deals with the fugue subjects, rather than with the ways in which they were treated later.

In order to follow the part-writing more clearly, the reader should transcribe the fugues, canons, etc. into open score. Besides being a useful exercise for the student of fugue, this alone gives a valuable insight into Beethoven's methods. The earnest student with less time at his disposal than this needs, should make and keep by him a copy of at least the motifs for each fugue as he studies it, since references to these are constantly made.

There are many editions of the Sonatas from which to choose in arriving at a basis for such transcriptions. Of these, Schenker's *Erläuterungsausgabe* is the best textual critical edition of the Sonatas, Opp. 101, 109, 110, and 111, because it is based on Beethoven's manuscripts. This edition was originally intended to include the Sonata, Op. 106, but Schenker did not discuss it because no autograph score is known to exist. Ferruccio Busoni has transcribed the fugal finale of this work into open score and given a detailed analysis. This forms one of the appendixes to his edition of Book I of *Das Wohltemperirte Clavier* and, apart from one or two small reservations, is admirable to use in conjunction with this study.

These publications by Schenker and Busoni are extremely difficult to obtain, and the reader will find that for the works they deal with, and for the remaining passages from the Sonatas, the complete edition in four volumes edited by Schenker and revised (1945) by his pupil Erwin Ratz, is the most authoritative and is easily obtainable.* All the Sonatas have been reconstrued according to the manuscripts where available and the first editions in other cases. Schenker follows in the minutest detail the exact manner in which Beethoven wrote his music, for instance, where a rising passage transfers from one stave to another, the correct placing of slurs and rests, the up or downward direction of stems, and so on. He felt that only in this way can one truly know Beethoven's style and fully appreciate the meaning of his music. The well-known Associated Board edition by Harold Craxton and Sir Donald F. Tovey† is generally reliable but it is not ultimately to be preferred to Schenker's.

As regards the Variations, there are comparatively few editions. None is ultimately reliable, but the text of the standard *Gesamtausgabe*, published by Breitkopf & Härtel, may be used, as there is no edition comparable with the work of Schenker and Busoni. The *Gesamtausgabe* is sometimes unreliable, because it was prepared by correctors who thought they knew better than Beethoven. Consequently, one should beware of gross unmusicalities in the phrasing when transcribing.

It is natural that a composer of Beethoven's stature should inspire many to write about his life and works. I acknowledge therefore, that in writing this study, I have been greatly indebted to a number of standard authorities. For the main, the works of Nottebohm, Schenker, and Busoni (already mentioned) have been drawn upon, together with frequent references to D. F. Tovey's *A Companion to Beethoven's Pianoforte Sonatas* and *Essays in Musical Analysis* and W. Nagel's *Beethoven und seine Klaviersonaten* (2nd edition), though the last of these does not generally add much to the others. H. Riemann's work, *L. van Beethoven's sämtliche Klaviersolosonaten* in three volumes, has not been accepted as an authority, because he introduced his own ideas about phrasing and even changed barlines according to his own system. Both his analyses and his editions are therefore unreliable.

Inevitably, the thirty-two Sonatas have attracted large numbers of writers throughout the years, but it is surprising that scarcely anything has been written about even the major

---

* *Ludwig van Beethoven: Klaviersonaten*, Universal-Edition, Vienna.
† *Beethoven: Sonatas for Pianoforte*, 3 vols., London, 1931.

sets of Variations, which are equally important in Beethoven's work. A critical edition of these works with detailed stylistic commentary is clearly called for.

In its original form this study was submitted as a thesis to the Board of the Faculty of Music in the University of Oxford for the degree of Bachelor of Letters. It has since been fundamentally revised and rewritten in the light of further research. Throughout all the work on this subject, I have received constant advice and encouragement from my research supervisor, Dr. Egon J. Wellesz. Many other people have helped me in various ways, especially by their patient and careful replies to my enquiries. Among these, my best thanks are due to Mr. V. Barwood, Miss Eleonore Breuning, a descendant of the Breuning family which befriended Beethoven, Mr. Adam Carse, Miss S. K. Cashin, Dr. Martin Cremer, Director of the Westdeutsche Bibliothek, Marburg, Dr. Otto Erich Deutsch, whose assistance was invaluable in the early stages, Dr. Frederick D. Dorian, of the Carnegie Institute of Technology, Pittsburgh, Mr. P. J. Frankis, Herr Willi Hess, the expert on Beethoven's works missing in the *Gesamtausgabe*, Mr. A. Hyatt King, Assistant Keeper, Department of Printed Books, British Museum, the late Dr. Georg Kinsky, Dr. Hedwig Kraus, Librarian of the Gesellschaft der Musikfreunde in Vienna, Dr. Krüger-Riebow, Director of the Music division of the Öffentliche Wissenschaftliche Bibliothek, formerly the Royal Library, and now the Deutsche Staatsbibliothek, Berlin, Colonel Donald W. MacArdle, the American scholar, whose extensive review (*Beethoven Abstracts*) of some 3,000 articles from several hundred periodicals as a preparation for the revision of Thayer's *The Life of Ludwig van Beethoven* is so valuable to the student of Beethoven, Professor Dr. Leopold Nowak, Director of the Music collection, Österreichische Nationalbibliothek, Vienna, Mr. C. B. Oldman, Principal Keeper, Department of Printed Books, British Museum, Herr von Reibnitz, Department of Berlin manuscripts, Universitätsbibliothek, Tübingen, Miss Sheila Rooke, who undertook a considerable amount of translation, Mr. L. G. D. Sanders, the late Dr. Percy A. Scholes, who very kindly allowed me to borrow books from his library for long periods, the late Miss Marion M. Scott, Mr. Jack Werner, and Herr Paul Wittgenstein.

Lastly, I must thank my Wife, Jeanette Cockshoot, who has given me much patient and devoted help and has read the whole book in typescript and been responsible for the proof-reading. Indeed, it is no exaggeration to say that her drive and enthusiasm have accelerated the production of this study in no small measure.

JOHN V. COCKSHOOT

I

THE CHIEF DEVELOPMENTS IN CONTRAPUNTAL THEORY BEFORE BEETHOVEN

BEFORE surveying Beethoven's essays in contrapuntal writing or even his studies in counterpoint and fugue under Haydn and Albrechtsberger, it is profitable to examine briefly the changing attitudes towards counterpoint in the sixteenth, seventeenth, and, especially, the eighteenth centuries. From this, it is possible to appreciate something of the background of musical thought against which Beethoven undertook his instruction as a young man, and the extent to which his later work is derived from it.

The age of Palestrina is a convenient starting-point. Palestrina was the most outstanding exponent of the *musica comuna* of the sixteenth century, a style which was the culmination of the musical developments and traditions of the past. Jeppeson speaks* of his art as being 'only slightly concerned with the new; the old is eternally new to it'. Theorists of the sixteenth century, however, in drawing up rules of counterpoint based on the Palestrina practice, enunciated only a few, compared with the possibilities. Jeppeson suggests† that this may have been because they lived too near Palestrina's own time to see his music in perspective, or that the theorists did not know some important rules or only partially disclosed their knowledge, or

* K. Jeppeson, *Counterpoint*, trans. by G. Haydon, New York, 1939, p. 23.
† Ibid., p. 24.

that certain aspects of contrapuntal technique were used in practice and not treated as matters of theory, possibly being 'secrets' passed on to pupils but not published. The treatises were rather attempts to describe the music than teaching manuals as we should understand them, and are valuable in what they accomplish.

In the later sixteenth century, the new *musica reservata* began to gain ground. This was intended to be more subjective and expressive than the traditional and objective *musica comuna*. It was developed and strengthened by the demands of the madrigal and the new notion of opera. Polyphony was giving way to homophony, dissonances were being treated more freely, and the modes were being moulded into major and minor scales. Yet, as Jeppeson shows,* seventeenth-century theorists, while extolling the new style for operas and madrigals, laid down the rule that, for sacred music, composers should use the old style. Accordingly, their contrapuntal rules are virtually those of the sixteenth century. Jeppeson's two explanations† of this devotion to these differing styles are unlikely. They are that (1) the theorists of the seventeenth century believed the new style somewhat unsuited for teaching purposes and (2) there is a tendency to inertia and resistance to change. The quotation which he gives from Berardi's treatise, *Miscellanea musicale* (1689),‡ shows that Berardi considered sixteenth-century composers were under a disadvantage in having to use essentially the same style of composition for sacred and secular works. The modern (seventeenth-century) composers, on the other hand, by reason of the later developments, had styles for religious, domestic, and theatre music, involving two techniques. For religious music the music was to be 'master of the text' (that is, contrapuntal), and for the domestic and dramatic music it was to be the 'servant of the text' (that is, harmonic). Surely, Berardi was asserting that contemporary composers had an advantage in the diversity of styles available to them. Far from resisting change, he was considering the Palestrina style ideal for sacred music, but not for secular music. Probably the idea that there ought to be a change had not occurred to him. He considered Palestrina 'the prince and father of music'. It was the secular

* Op. cit., pp. 34 f.
† Ibid., p. 35.   ‡ Ibid., loc. cit.

music that needed, and had undergone, change, to his evident satisfaction.

The contribution of the seventeenth-century theorists was their evolution of a system of teaching counterpoint, rather than of describing it. They no longer reproduced passages from the great masters for imitation, but worked out special exercises to show particular difficulties of technique. The *cantus firmus* and the system of 'species' were the basis of their teaching methods, and these survive today.

Diruta's *Il Transilvano* (1597) seems to be the first treatise that uses the five species, though not in the usual order. Banchieri's *Cartella musicale* (1614) deals with the first four species and then adds other contrapuntal disciplines. The five species are treated in the familiar order in Zacconi's *Prattica di musica* (1622), which includes still more species. Jeppeson speaks* of Berardi's power of inventing new species as 'almost inexhaustible'. The contrapuntal rules and exercises, though arranged for teaching purposes, were becoming superfluous and trifling in their number and quality, until Fux established a definitive set of five species and graded the difficulties in using them, in his famous *Gradus ad Parnassum* (1725).

Fux wrote his book at the age of sixty-five, after a lifetime of teaching experience. He confessedly takes Palestrina as his model, but it must not be thought that his book is a true picture of that style. Jeppeson gives† three reasons for this: (1) Palestrina's works were not then generally available and Fux knew comparatively few, (2) the previous Italian theorists, on whom Fux relied, taught counterpoint more from a harmonic point of view, and (3) Fux unconsciously introduced contemporary musical idioms into his own work. The value of Jeppeson's book is that it has the virtues of Fux's methods of treatment, but is free of the foregoing disadvantages.

The *Gradus ad Parnassum* was published at the Emperor Charles VI's expense and was soon sold out and distributed widely. It was written in Latin (rather than in a vernacular), and thus its wide acceptance was assured. Translations were soon made, the first being by Telemann. The book consisted firstly of a section on the divisions, arithmetical and harmonic, of the octave, and similar acoustical problems, common to the

* Ibid., p. 41.　　　　　† Ibid., Preface, p. xiv.

treatises of the period. The main, instructional part of the book is in the classical form of a dialogue between the pupil (Josephus) and the master (Aloysius), that is, Fux's version of Palestrina. It is divided into two parts, devoted to the study of counterpoint and the study of the fugue, both of which have been translated* authoritatively by Alfred Mann, who has added explanatory footnotes.

Fux begins the study of counterpoint with two-part writing, in which the five species are successively introduced. In each of the species, the examples shown as worked by the pupil are graded in difficulty. Mistakes made by the pupil are discussed, and these are often anticipated by the master. The process is repeated for three-part writing and again for four-part writing. For his *cantus firmi* Fux uses the old ecclesiastical modes, and sharps and flats are limited to cadences and the avoidance of tritones.

The study of the fugue begins with a short section on imitation, followed by another on fugues in general and the use of the modes in them. Fux then begins a discussion of fugues in two voices, with an example for each of the six modes, based on D, E, F, G, A, and C, as before. The same procedure is then followed for fugues in three voices, and again for fugues in four voices, though examples of the latter are given only in the modes of D, E, and F. Josephus has made such good progress that Aloysius allows him to work out fugues in the other modes by himself, so that he (Aloysius) can pass on to a discussion of double counterpoint, preparatory to dealing with fugues with several themes. Double counterpoint is treated successively at the octave, tenth, and twelfth. This done, Josephus is reminded of the restrictions of the *cantus firmus* and the diatonic system of the modes. He is now free, armed with a perfect command of his art, to choose his own subject, use chromaticisms, all kinds of time-signatures, smaller note-values, themes requiring tonal answers, and transposed modes. An example of a fugue with three subjects is given, and with this, Alfred Mann's translation

* (a) The study of counterpoint: J. J. Fux, *Steps to Parnassus*, trans. and ed. by A. Mann, New York, 1943. (b) The study of the fugue: J. J. Fux, 'The Study of the Fugue: A Dialogue', trans. and ed. by A. Mann, *Musical Quarterly*, XXXVI, 525–39 (October 1950), XXXVII, 28–44 (January 1951), 203–19 (April 1951), and 376–93 (July 1951).

ends. Fux goes on, however, with other matters, with headings as follow: *De Figura Variationis, & Anticipationis, De Modis, De variis Fugarum Subjectis, De Gustu, De Stylo Ecclesiastico, De Stylo à Capella, De Stylo Mixto,* and *De Stylo recitativo.*

Some idea of the differences between Fux's interpretation of Palestrina's style and the style as it actually is can be gained from examples mentioned by Jeppeson (Exx. 1–8). Fux says* that, in third species, the third crotchet may be dissonant if the second and fourth crotchets are consonant (Ex. 1). Jeppeson does not know† where Fux found this rule and suggests he may have formulated it himself; it is not based on Palestrina's style. Fux goes on to show‡ that they are merely fillings-in of skips of a third and gives their original forms (Ex. 2). This space

Ex. 1

6 5 4 3   5 6 7 8   3 5 4 3   8 6 7 8   3 1 2 3   3 5 4 3

Ex. 2

Ex. 3

Fux

Ad   te   Do   mi-ne   le - va _ _ _ _ _

Palestrina

---

* *Steps to Parnassus*, p. 50. (*Gradus ad Parnassum*, Vienna, 1725, p. 64.)
† Op. cit., p. 40.
‡ *Steps to Parnassus*, pp. 50 f. (*Gradus ad Parnassum*, p. 64.)

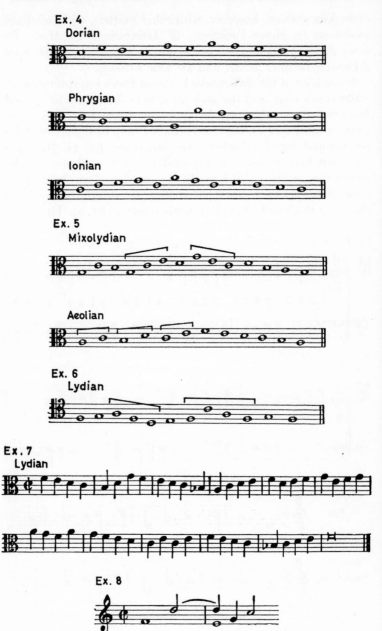

from the second to the third note, Fux says, can always be filled in.

Jeppeson contrasts* a theme from a motet by Fux with one from Palestrina's motet *Surge propera*, which has the same order of notes (Ex. 3). Because bar 3 repeats bar 2 rhythmically at a higher level and the first note of this rhythm is the highest note so far in the melody in each case, Fux's theme is sharp and exuberant in effect, and completely different from the gentle, horizontal style of Palestrina's theme. Jeppeson approves of Fux's theme in itself, but not as an essay in Palestrina's style. However, as this was not used in the *Gradus ad Parnassum* we are not justified in expecting that all Fux's church music should keep to the precepts of Palestrina's style, even if he had fully understood it. We know that Fux, as a practising composer, did not faithfully keep to the 'rules', but used the study of counterpoint only as an aid to mastery in composition.

Even the *cantus firmi* must be composed and considered melodically; there must be no suggestion of any implied harmony. In drawing up suitable *cantus firmi* in the various modes, Jeppeson accepts† three of those composed by Fux (Ex. 4), but rejects those in the Mixolydian and Aeolian modes (Ex. 5). In the Mixolydian example chords are implied where indicated with square brackets. Jeppeson warns‡ against constant skipping and triviality in sequences, as shown in the Aeolian example, and adds that the beginning suggests broken chords. Jeppeson discards§ the Lydian mode as being coincidental with the Ionian in polyphonic practice, but he would certainly have disapproved of Fux's Lydian *cantus firmus* on account of its chordal implications (Ex. 6).

An example of a melody from Fux, quoted by Jeppeson,‖ shows how harmonic considerations have preponderated,

* Op. cit., pp. 95 f.

† Ibid., pp. 107 f. A misprint occurs in Jeppeson's footnote (p. 107): those *cantus firmi* by Fux which he uses are numbers 1, 6, and 19, not 1, 6, and 20.

‡ Ibid., p. 111.

§ Ibid., p. 107.

‖ Ibid., pp. 122 f. Jeppeson's aim (p. 122), 'to demonstrate the contrast between the older counterpoint, more harmonically based and the newer of stronger melodic tendencies', should surely read that the older counterpoint was more *melodically* based and the newer had stronger *harmonic* tendencies.

7

though marked linear features are clearly evident (Ex. 7). Bar 2 contains a $^6_3$ chord of G, and skips in the same direction in crotchet movement are never found in Palestrina. Bars 5-7 are fundamentally harmonic progressions. Bar 9 has a sequence and is awkward. More importantly, there should be no upward skip from an accented crotchet. This fault occurs also in bars 2, 4, and 7.

Jeppeson quotes* one of Fux's examples of a decorated re-solution (Ex. 8). This figure was certainly used by the more progressive composers of the English Madrigal School but not by Palestrina. It became more common by the beginning of the eighteenth century and therefore it seems that Fux was using an idiom from contemporary music.

A fugue is reproduced† in Jeppeson's book which, by its strict retention of a countersubject throughout, is virtually a double fugue. This form is alien to the sixteenth century and belongs to the eighteenth.

Despite its unsatisfactoriness as an exposition of the Palestrina style of counterpoint, the *Gradus ad Parnassum* has exercised an incalculable influence in contrapuntal teaching and the training of composers ever since its publication in 1725. Alfred Mann gives‡ an outline of this influence, the extent of which can be gauged by the prominence in musical history of those who taught or learned from it.

He concludes that Bach recognized Fux's method, for his pupil, L. C. Mizler (1711-78), made a translation under his supervision. In fact, C. P. E. Bach, in a letter from Hamburg dated 13th January 1775 to the German scholar, J. N. Forkel, stated that his father esteemed Fux highly in his last years, though he did not know him personally.§ Leopold Mozart's name appears in a copy. Padre G. B. Martini (1706-84), who taught W. A. Mozart, used no other system, and Mozart's workings of Fux's exercises exist. Haydn praised the book, worked the exercises, and revised his workings, also making an

* Op. cit., p. 148.
† Ibid., pp. 277-80.
‡ J. J. Fux, *Steps to Parnassus*, pp. 7-9. This outline is part of 'A Note on the History of the *Gradus ad Parnassum*' by the translator and editor, A. Mann, which precedes the translation.
§ H. T. David and A. Mendel, eds., *The Bach Reader*, 1945, p. 279.

abstract of the book. Beethoven studied from this abstract, and himself made another.

Besides teaching Fux's system to Beethoven, J. G. Albrechtsberger (1736–1809) taught Ignaz Ritter von Seyfried (1776–1841) who was also a pupil of Haydn. E. Marxsen (1806–87), Seyfried's pupil, used the system to teach Brahms. Fétis's translation (1833) of Seyfried's edition of Beethoven's studies was subscribed for by a number of famous composers. The edition, though very unreliable, revived and intensified interest in counterpoint.

C. F. Zelter (1758–1832) taught Fux's system to Mendelssohn, who taught M. G. Nottebohm (1817–82), and it was passed on to E. Mandyczewski (1857–1929), and Scalero (q. 1870). Bruckner also based his teaching on Fux.

At the present time, K. Jeppeson (b. 1892) acknowledges the greatness of Fux's work, but purges it of all features that do not conform to Palestrina's style in his *Counterpoint*. Hindemith (b. 1895), too, testifies to the eminence of the *Gradus ad Parnassum* in his *Craft of Musical Composition* (Vol. I).

While the theory of counterpoint which presupposed the writing of melodic lines and rhythms was being evolved, culminating in Fux's work, musical practice was developing quickly along harmonic lines with the advent of the thoroughbass. The realization of thoroughbass brought with it a theory of harmony which, when fully understood, could be made the starting-point and basis of counterpoint. Instead of counterpoint's being founded on melody, it can now be conceived harmonically.

This was the method and teaching of no less a composer than Bach. Bach did not write any theoretical treatise, but his ardent pupil, J. P. Kirnberger, tried to set down his teachings and may fairly be said to have done so in his *Die Kunst des reinen Satzes in der Musik* (1771–9). For Kirnberger, as Jeppeson points out,* Bach's style alone is valid. Kirnberger finds that Fux's rules are too strict and that he goes on to fugue too soon.

The first volume opens with the customary acoustical section, and goes on to sections on intervals, chords, and triads. Kirnberger deals in turn with dissonances, cadences, modulation to near and remote keys, sudden modulations, and consonant and

* Op. cit., p. 43.

dissonant melodic skips. Only then does he turn his attention to counterpoint. But the chord is fundamental, and intervals are all related to the parts they can play in chords. Kirnberger therefore starts the contrapuntal section with four-part counterpoint in first species, leading to counterpoint in three parts and then in two parts. Two-part writing is left to the last, because harmonically the chords formed thereby are incomplete. To write in four parts with complete chords is considered much easier.

After dealing with five- and six-part writing, Kirnberger reaches the equivalent of fifth species. Essential differences between the Bach and Palestrina styles are evident here. In treating this fifth species, or florid counterpoint, he admits chordal figuration, not used in the sixteenth century. Unaccented, or 'regular', passing notes can now be approached and quitted by step. 'Irregular', or accented passing notes are introduced. Kirnberger recommends Graun's music for study in this matter, rather than that of Bach or Handel, because Graun is prudent and Bach, by being bolder, has some harsh effects. These harshnesses are caused by the independence of the horizontal lines at certain points, in spite of the radically vertical approach to the music, and Kirnberger recognizes this. Finally, he deals with syncopation of the fourth-species type in florid counterpoint.

The second part of Kirnberger's work is less relevant to contrapuntal theory, once he has considered the old modes and modern scales and has stated that a good and flowing melody must be based on correct harmonies. Seconds and thirds are recommended as intervals in ordinary melodies; larger ones should be reserved for accentuation or special emotions, which leads to a catalogue of the various emotions suggested by each interval.

Later sections of the treatise discuss metre, rhythm, and double counterpoint, again with a harmonic background.

Jeppeson feels* that Kirnberger, though thorough and able, made very little of Bach's polyphonic genius, but it serves as a useful guide to Bach's own teaching method. Not until a century had elapsed was Kirnberger's work continued—in 1872 by Richter. Meanwhile, Fux held sway in the contrapuntal

* Op. cit., p. 47.

field (Rameau's *Traité de l'harmonie* (1722) represented the real progress in the theory of harmony) and it was Fux's influence under which Beethoven came so strongly during the period of his studies.

II

BEETHOVEN'S CONTRAPUNTAL
AND FUGAL STUDIES

Seyfried and Nottebohm

Very soon after Beethoven's death, interest in his studies was aroused when, in the auction of the composer's musical effects in November 1827, lot No. 149: 'Contrapunktische Aufsätze, 5 Pakete' was offered for sale. Tobias Haslinger, the Viennese publisher so often referred to as the Adjutant in the imaginary military organization in Beethoven's correspondence, was the purchaser. He handed the five packets to Ignaz Ritter von Seyfried for compilation with a view to publication.

Seyfried had, like Beethoven, been a pupil of Haydn and Albrechtsberger, and should have been ideal for this work. His compilation was published by Haslinger in 1832 under the title *Ludwig van Beethoven's Studien im Generalbasse, Contrapuncte und in der Compositionslehre*. Some regarded it as authentic and others as a complete forgery.

The original packets passed to Haslinger's daughter-in-law, who allowed Nottebohm to make a detailed revision of the contents, which, after the passage of some forty years, were somewhat less complete. They were, however, complete enough for Nottebohm to make some important discoveries about Seyfried's book and he published his findings in his *Beethoveniana*.* These show that Seyfried did the most amazing things.

* G. Nottebohm, 'Generalbass und Compositionslehre betreffende Handschriften Beethoven's und J. R. v. Seyfried's Buch "Ludwig van Beethoven's

For instance, one packet contained, *inter alia*, Beethoven's *Materialien zum Generalbass*, a kind of manual which the composer prepared from the 2nd Part of C. P. E. Bach's *Versuch über die wahre Art das Clavier zu spielen* in the improved 2nd edition of 1797, the 1st edition of D. G. Türk's *Kurze Anweisung zum Generalbassspielen* (1791), the 1st edition of J. G. Albrechtsberger's *Gründliche Anweisung zur Composition* (1790), and J. P. Kirnberger's *Die Kunst des reinen Satzes in der Musik* (Vienna edition), all of which were standard text-books of the period. From external evidence, Nottebohm was able to date the writing of the manual as the second quarter of 1809. Nottebohm quotes* word for word the text of the opening pages of the *Materialien zum Generalbass*, and this quotation is equivalent to Seyfried's first chapter. A comparison with Seyfried's version shows that Seyfried left no sentence unaltered. The same happened with the music examples: notes were altered in value, left out, or added.

A somewhat similar fate befell the transcription made by Beethoven, principally of sections of the *Gradus ad Parnassum* in L. Mizler's German translation (1742), under the heading *Einleitung zur Fuxischen Lehre vom Kontrapunkt*. From the nature of the handwriting, similarity of the paper, etc. this was also certainly written in 1809. Seyfried shows a fundamental misconception of the purpose of Beethoven's two compilations in including them in a book on Beethoven's studies. They were intended as teaching material and were very probably occasioned by Beethoven's instruction of his friend and patron, the Archduke Rudolf, who had become his pupil about this time. The Archduke was obliged to leave Vienna from May 1809 to January 1810 during the French siege and occupation of the city, and Nottebohm suggests† that Beethoven used his absence to write down these extracts in order to be better prepared for a possibly prolonged resumption of the instruction on the Archduke's return. Nottebohm demonstrates the rough treatment which Seyfried meted out to the other manuscripts. When he deals with Beethoven's exercises worked for Haydn and Albrechtsberger, Nottebohm gives catalogues of the falsifica-

Studien im Generalbasse, Contrapuncte" u.s.w.', *Beethoveniana*, 1872, pp. 154–203.
* Ibid., pp. 156 ff.   † Ibid., p. 202.

tions which Seyfried introduced into his transcriptions. Seyfried is shown to have added comments and figuring, and changed, added, or omitted notes.

Nottebohm's findings are merciless in their attack on Seyfried's book, which is scornfully dismissed in his final paragraph. The more positive outcome of this research was Nottebohm's *Beethoven's Studien*, which appeared in 1873, and gives an accurate and absorbing account of Beethoven's studies principally with Haydn, Albrechtsberger, and Salieri. It was to have been followed by another volume devoted to Beethoven's own independent studies, but this was never published.

Studies at Bonn

Beethoven's only teacher at Bonn who merits attention is Christian Gottlob Neefe (1748–98). He came to Bonn in 1779 and was court organist from 1783. In a preliminary section of his book, Nottebohm conjectures* an assessment of the value to Beethoven of his studies with Neefe.

Nottebohm reproduces† Neefe's famous entry in Cramer's *Magazin der Musik* of 2nd March 1783, which speaks of Beethoven's playing Bach's *Das Wohltemperirte Clavier* and learning thoroughbass and composition. The instruction in thoroughbass was based on the teaching Neefe had had from J. A. Hiller and on Kirnberger's text-books. By 'composition' was meant simple counterpoint, imitation, fugue, etc., which meaning is intended in the titles of contemporary manuals, such as Marpurg's *Handbuch bey dem Generalbasse und der Composition* (1755–8) and Albrechtsberger's *Gründliche Anweisung zur Composition* (1790).

In view of Neefe's own musical education and his work as a theatre composer, Nottebohm considers‡ it impossible that he devised exercises in strict counterpoint, but rather that he used standard text-books, e.g., those of Marpurg and Kirnberger, though which book or books one cannot say, even if it is certain that he did use one. No exercises are extant, and Beethoven's early compositions must indicate any progress in counterpoint. The Variations on a March by Dressler show no independence

* 'Bonner Studien', *Beethoven's Studien*, 1873, pp. 1–18.
† Ibid., pp. 4 f.　　　　　　　　‡ Ibid., p. 9.

14

in part-writing. The three Sonatas for pianoforte (1783) have occasional glimpses of it. A two-part organ fugue (1783) displays much essentially independent part-writing, though the incorrect treatment of a fourth at one point shows faulty tuition in Nottebohm's opinion.*

Progress can be seen in the three Pianoforte Quartets (1785), the Prelude in F minor for pianoforte (1785 or 1787), the two Preludes through all the major keys, Op. 39 (1789), and the Variations on Righini's Arietta *Venni amore* (1790). Points of imitation occur in these latter works. This might correspond to instruction in handling imitation which usually follows strict counterpoint in the text-books.

A Mozartian influence in the style of figuration and the formation of motifs can be detected in Beethoven's compositions between 1785 and 1792. Figuration is an important factor in helping the accompanying parts to acquire their own characteristics and fulfil independent functions in the music.

Beethoven's playing of Bach's fugues does not mean he was well versed in the technicalities of writing a fugue, as the errors in his fugues written for Albrechtsberger show. His two-part organ fugue of 1783 shows, however, that he had assimilated the essence of fugue, and could maintain a theme and develop it freely. Nottebohm believes† that Beethoven could have learned nothing in Bonn about double counterpoint according to the rules, and his exercises for Albrechtsberger show this too. The fundamental reason for these gaps in Beethoven's instruction can be traced to the taste of the time, which sought simplicity and mostly avoided complex polyphony. Neefe's own musical education was unbalanced to the neglect of counterpoint. In his compositions he avoided fugue; even in his sacred works, where polyphony was traditionally most suitable, he sought the simple style.

Neefe, however, was a man of aesthetic sensibility and wrote on psychology and aesthetics in music, which must have had a great influence on Beethoven's mental development during his most impressionable years.

Nottebohm concludes‡ that Beethoven's instruction from Neefe was insufficient technically, but that, as regards the

---

* Ibid., pp. 10 ff.   † Ibid., p. 14.
‡ Ibid., p. 18.

formation of taste and development of musical feeling, his influence could have been only beneficial and lasting.

Studies with Haydn

Beethoven went to Vienna in 1787 and met Mozart. It is not certain that he had any instruction in counterpoint from him and there are no exercises in known existence. Beethoven was in Vienna such a short time that it is doubtful if anything substantial could have been accomplished.

Later, in December 1790 and July 1792, Beethoven met Haydn as he passed through Bonn on his first journey to and from England. Following on the interest which Haydn showed in Beethoven's work, it was decided to send him to Vienna to study with Haydn. Beethoven arrived in Vienna in November 1792 and the instruction began shortly afterwards.

Haydn greatly valued Fux's *Gradus ad Parnassum* and made an abstract of the rules of strict counterpoint from it and from other text-books such as those of C. P. E. Bach and Kirnberger. Beethoven's copy of this abstract has been lost, but Nottebohm reconstructs* it from two other copies, one incomplete and the other unreliable.

At the time of Nottebohm's investigation, 245 of Beethoven's exercises for Haydn existed out of a probable total of some 300. Forty-two exercises bear marks of correction by Haydn, and Nottebohm quotes these, together with six others. Nowhere does Haydn add a reason or say what rule is broken in his corrections, though Nottebohm adds the necessary explanations. All the exercises are concerned with counterpoint in the five species in two-, three-, and four-part writing.

Even in the comparatively few exercises which carry any mark of Haydn's supervision, some surprising things happen. In correcting one error, Haydn often makes another in his solution. Examples of consecutive fifths and octaves are passed unmarked. Sometimes, he finds hidden fifths but misses consecutive fifths in the same exercise. In one exercise, Haydn even alters the *cantus firmus* in his correction. In another, Haydn's correction introduces a leap of a seventh. This, and the overlooking of a seventh which was improperly treated, suggest that

* 'Unterricht bei Joseph Haydn', *Beethoven's Studien*, pp. 21 ff.

Haydn, in Nottebohm's view*, was not completely familiar with the requirements of strict counterpoint. More likely, Haydn either had been familiar with these requirements, but at the age of sixty had long since ceased to practise them in composition, or was now, a celebrated composer, too busy to care sufficiently about his pupil's work.

One can only conclude with Nottebohm† that Haydn was not a systematic, fundamental, or strict teacher. As only a sixth of the exercises show any trace at all of Haydn's supervision, one can reasonably assume that he was hasty and uninterested in Beethoven's work. Little wonder that Beethoven was dissatisfied with his progress. Thayer quotes‡ the well-known passage from the autobiography of Johann Schenk (1753–1836), an opera composer, which tells how, at the instance of the Abbé Gelinek, Beethoven became his secret pupil. Schenk had seen the errors in Beethoven's exercises, and gave him Fux's book together with exercises to work. These were marked by Schenk and fair copies of the corrected work made by Beethoven, so that Haydn should not detect unfamiliar writing.

Schenk's autobiography was written many years later, and his recollections, especially about the dates of this instruction, are vague. It is generally accepted, however, that it lasted from August 1793 to May 1794. Haydn left for England again on 19th January 1794 and Beethoven was handed over to Albrechtsberger. As Schenk does not seem to have objected to Albrechtsberger, it is strange that he should have thought it necessary to continue teaching Beethoven, once Haydn had departed. No exercises done for Schenk are however available.

Studies with Albrechtsberger

Beethoven worked with Albrechtsberger for rather more than a year, according to Nottebohm.§ Thayer suggests‖ that Beethoven finished between March and May 1795.

* Ibid., p. 42.
† Ibid., p. 43.
‡ A. W. Thayer, *The Life of Ludwig van Beethoven*, revised and amended by H. E. Krehbiel, 1921, I, 153 f.
§ 'Generalbass und Compositionslehre, etc.', *Beethoveniana*, p. 198.
‖ Op. cit., I, 160.

The studies consisted of strict counterpoint, counterpoint in a freer style, imitation, two-, three-, and four-part fugues, fugues on a chorale, double counterpoint at the octave, tenth, and twelfth, double fugue, triple counterpoint at the octave, triple fugue, and canon. Albrechtsberger taught from his own book, *Gründliche Anweisung zur Composition* (1790), which is based on Fux, with the chief difference that the major and minor keys of the new music are introduced instead of the old modes.

Beethoven went right back to first principles with Albrechtsberger. It may well be that Beethoven showed him all his work for Haydn and, seeing Haydn's unsatisfactory corrections, Albrechtsberger thought this course necessary. Nottebohm gives evidence of Albrechtsberger's adding remarks on some of the exercises actually written for Haydn,* and the new teacher gives new rules which forbid an octave on a beat, major and dissonant leaps, and ordain that the fourth degree of the major scale should fall a semitone and the seventh degree rise, together with a demonstration of the use of the tritone (referred to in those days as *mi contra fa*). Beethoven thereupon worked no less than 125 exercises in two-, three-, and four-part strict counterpoint in the various species, using *cantus firmi* in F major and D minor.

In the exercises in the freer contrapuntal style suitable to church, chamber, and theatre, Albrechtsberger allows several liberties in treatment, such as leaps which make a dissonant interval, chromatic progressions, unprepared sevenths, diminished chords, and much else besides. These ideas are a further deviation from Fux and a still further deviation from the Palestrina style. The harmonic aspects of the counterpoint are being stressed more and more, and suit the tastes of the time. Beethoven worked twenty-six examples of this type which, in spite of their free style of melody and harmony, are worked in the five species of strict counterpoint.

In all this work, Beethoven had, according to Nottebohm,† used great care and tried to keep to the rules and avoid errors. Albrechtsberger generally corrected carefully and fully. Nottebohm gives‡ as an example of Beethoven's willingness and the

---

* 'Unterricht bei J. G. Albrechtsberger', *Beethoven's Studien*, pp. 47 f.
† *Beethoven's Studien*, p. 196.
‡ Ibid., loc. cit.

understanding between teacher and pupil the query 'ist es erlaubt?' (is it allowed?), which Beethoven wrote on one of his exercises.

There are no small exercises in imitation in existence, but instead three preludes to fugues, written for strings, two of which show a proficiency in the handling of imitation. These are written with great care and in a free instrumental style, with no reference to strict counterpoint. Albrechtsberger's corrections are shown in the only prelude that is quoted by Nottebohm. * Beethoven himself revised this fugue and his further alterations are given;† they do not coincide with Albrechtsberger's corrections and even concern bars which were previously correct and Albrechtsberger had passed. Sometimes, Beethoven's alterations are an improvement on Albrechtsberger's suggestions.

The next stage in the instruction brings Beethoven to two-part fugue. Nottebohm gives‡ Albrechtsberger's rules for the layout of a simple two-part fugue. These are based very closely on Fux§ and Albrechtsberger expands them a little. A fugue is in three sections, and in each section each voice has the theme at least once. Subject and answer act as tonic and dominant to each other and vice versa. If the subject begins on the tonic, the answer begins on the dominant, etc. Each fugue theme must be capable of two *stretti*, a half *stretto* (*semirestrictio*) and a whole *stretto* (*restrictio*). The former is set in the second section and the latter in the third section of the fugue. In practice, irrespective of the length of the subject, the *semirestrictio* is a *stretto* at two bars' distance which is narrowed to one bar for the *restrictio*. Each of the three sections ends with a cadence in fourth or fifth species and in the dominant, mediant, and tonic respectively. The place of an episode, or 'free modulation', is laid down and the voice which should begin it. The voice accompanying the subject‖ must be in the fifth species of strict counterpoint, and the use of ties causing dissonances is recommended.

---

* Ibid., pp. 63 ff.   † Ibid., p. 68.   ‡ Ibid., pp. 70 f.

§ J. J. Fux, 'The Study of the Fugue: A Dialogue—I', trans. and ed. by A. Mann, *Musical Quarterly*, XXXVI, 531 f. (October 1950). (*Gradus ad Parnassum*, p. 146.)

‖ German: Gegenharmonie (Gegensatz). It cannot logically be called a countersubject because it is not a permanent feature, even in three- and four-part fugues.

To these rules, Albrechtsberger adds a collection of thirty fugue subjects under the heading *Fugarum Themata ad Semi-restrictionem et Restrictionem apta*. They are, therefore, suitable for both half and whole *stretto*, and Beethoven used them to the end of his instruction with Albrechtsberger. These rules and fugue subjects show that Albrechtsberger taught fugue as an extension of counterpoint, a kind of *contrappunto fugato*, as Nottebohm puts it,★ so that two-part fugues are written according to the rules of two-part strict counterpoint, three-part fugues according to the rules of three-part strict counterpoint, and so on. If the accompanying voice is to be in fifth species, there tends to be an insufficient distinction between it and the subject. Nottebohm says† that the fifth species is not a magic book from which to choose everything, and avers that it leads to a limitation of the accompanying harmony and a neglect of the episodes. In his view it spoiled Beethoven's work.

Beethoven wrote thirty-eight fugues of different kinds, using Albrechtsberger's subjects. Of these, eighteen are two-part fugues, and before working them he often sketched the *stretti*. These fugues are not always well done according to Albrechtsberger's wishes. Fundamental mistakes like hidden fifths and octaves recur, and there are some cases of incorrect answers to the subjects, both in the miniature expositions and in the *stretti*, which are duly corrected. The usual fault is that tonic is not answered by dominant and vice versa. Improvements made by Albrechtsberger concentrate on a greater use of suspension and rhythmical interest.

Of three-part fugues, Beethoven wrote seven, together with the one in free style for strings, mentioned earlier. Here again, signs of carelessness creep in. Nottebohm shows‡ Albrechtsberger altering one accompanying voice set in third species to make it conform to fifth species, and in another case,§ Beethoven altering the theme in the answer, but these and other mistakes in this fugue Albrechtsberger has not marked: he made two purely minor amendments near the end.

Beethoven wrote nine four-part fugues in the same strict style. Nottebohm wonders‖ whether Beethoven worked the strict fugues unwillingly. The models put before him and Albrechts-

★ *Beethoven's Studien*, p. 195.   † Ibid., p. 196.   ‡ Ibid., p. 91.
§ Ibid., p. 93.   ‖ Ibid., p. 196.

berger's constricting rules could say nothing to Beethoven, and would make him weary of the 'art of making musical skeletons'.* In one fugue,† Beethoven writes the answer in two successive entries, instead of maintaining an alternation of subject and answer. Albrechtsberger allows‡ Beethoven's incorrect answer in another fugue.

Fugues on a chorale follow next, and Albrechtsberger's rules are given. Beethoven wrote three of these. For the former of the two quoted by Nottebohm, Albrechtsberger writes§ the chorale, the fugue theme formed from it, and lastly a *stretto*. Beethoven set to work on the fugue, but seems to have had trouble and he left it incomplete after fifty-three bars. Albrechtsberger began to correct it, but this involved such basic alterations that he rewrote Beethoven's work from bar 23 and continued it to about bar 80. Then, having seen how the motifs, which imitate the chorale, are passed through each part, Beethoven added another forty-five bars, no doubt under Albrechtsberger's supervision. Before the second fugue, Albrechtsberger also wrote the chorale and the subject in *stretto*. Errors of part-writing constantly occur and Beethoven does not eliminate them in succeeding fugues. Nottebohm even thinks‖ that the counterpoint is worse in the three- and four-part fugues than in the contrapuntal exercises.

In contrast, Beethoven's exercises in double counterpoint are done with great care and are free from big mistakes, and probably result from better instruction. However, Beethoven still makes mistakes, which suggest that the idea of double counterpoint was new to him.

Albrechtsberger explains with some examples double counterpoint at the octave but does not deal with the difficulty of inverting the fifth, and Beethoven makes an extract for himself from Kirnberger's *Die Kunst des reinen Satzes in der Musik* which deals with the matter more fully. Albrechtsberger does show, however, how the simultaneous addition at the interval of a tenth of one or both parts makes effective three- and four-part

---

* *Beethoven: the Man and the Artist, as revealed in his own words*, compiled by F. Kerst, trans. by H. E. Krehbiel, 1926, p. 25.

† *Beethoven's Studien*, p. 95. This fugue is discussed further in Chapter III, p. 30.

‡ Ibid., p. 100.   § Ibid., pp. 112 ff.   ‖ Ibid., p. 196.

writing, when the two parts have a unison, third, sixth, or an octave on an accented part of the bar. This use of parallel motion is typical of Fux's teaching* and can be seen freely used by Beethoven in the fugues to be discussed in later chapters. Incidentally, Albrechtsberger's own example has consecutive octaves three bars from the end.† Beethoven follows his work on double counterpoint at the octave with some exercises, including two at the fifteenth. Albrechtsberger then supplies a fugue theme, sketched in *stretto*, and Beethoven, after working out a countersubject, writes an extensive fugue of 103 bars for string quartet, a feature of which is a pedal of eight bars. Nottebohm reproduces‡ it in full. The subject opens with a leap from tonic to dominant, which Beethoven answers incorrectly from dominant to supertonic. Albrechtsberger does not correct this, but makes necessary amendments of many of the numerous faults in part-writing.

Albrechtsberger explains double counterpoint at the tenth in detail, in which Beethoven works twenty-four exercises. A semibreve *cantus firmus* is used for some of the exercises, but in others both voices are in fifth species. Sometimes three- and four-part texture is achieved by the addition of one or two parts which are either free or run in parallel tenths with the original voices in the manner mentioned in the paragraph above. The parallel writing makes for an enrichment of the texture without complicating the counterpoint and also provides a simultaneous presentation of the original form and the inversion. Fewer mistakes appear in Beethoven's work at this point.

As a final preparation for writing double fugues, Beethoven now takes up double counterpoint at the twelfth. This is also fully explained with examples by Albrechtsberger, whereupon Beethoven works six exercises. In one case,§ Beethoven writes a twelfth (which would invert as a unison) on an accent. Surprisingly, Albrechtsberger alters the *cantus firmus* and, in doing so, widens the twelfth by a third, so that no inversion is possible.

---

* J. J. Fux, 'The Study of the Fugue: A Dialogue—III', trans. and ed. by A. Mann, *Musical Quarterly*, XXXVII, 207 ff. (April 1951). (*Gradus ad Parnassum*, pp. 179 ff.)

† G. Nottebohm, 'Unterricht bei J. G. Albrechtsberger', *Beethoven's Studien*, p. 128.

‡ Ibid., pp. 132 ff. § Ibid., p. 149.

Albrechtsberger distinguishes between the two kinds of double fugue, in which the two subjects can be introduced either simultaneously or separately. The rules relating to simple fugues are to be kept as far as possible, but Albrechtsberger gives his rules for making necessary deviations in dealing with two themes. Beethoven attempts six double fugues of both kinds. In the first which Nottebohm reproduces,* Beethoven gives the two simultaneous subjects to the soprano and alto. The answers in the dominant are given to the same two voices as an inversion of the subjects. As a result there is only two-part writing until the third entry, when the tenor and bass enter together with the subjects. Albrechtsberger alters the opening, to give the 1st subject to the soprano and the 2nd subject to the bass. He then gives the answer of the 1st subject to the alto, while the soprano retains the answer of the 2nd and the bass continues as a free part. It is noteworthy that, in the double fugue (Variation XXXII) of the Thirty-three Variations on a Waltz of Diabelli, Op. 120, Beethoven again begins with the two subjects in the soprano and alto, but, as if in defiance of Albrechtsberger, solves the problem by giving the answers to the tenor and bass. Beethoven's double fugue for Albrechtsberger lacks any *stretto*, and parallel part-writing, though constantly used, lacks variety in being confined to a coupling of soprano with tenor and alto with bass. It seems as if Beethoven was becoming somewhat bored with the work, for Albrechtsberger has henceforth to help him in greater or less degree.

Teacher and pupil write the second fugue together,† wherein Albrechtsberger helps and advises. All the technical devices taught so far are introduced, and scarcely a mistake is made. Albrechtsberger helps with another fugue and then gives Beethoven the two simultaneous subjects for a double fugue for string quartet in free style to work by himself. However, many mistakes of the most basic kind occur, such as consecutive and hidden fifths and octaves, which Nottebohm, as usual, catalogues thoroughly.‡ The next fugue§ shows Beethoven confining both subjects and answers to only the soprano and alto, as in the first fugue. Beethoven has not learned his lesson, but one wonders whether he was interested enough to do so now.

* Ibid., pp. 152 ff.   † Ibid., pp. 155 ff.
‡ Ibid., pp. 166 f.   § Ibid., pp. 167 ff.

Beethoven seems to have so much trouble with this type of double fugue, especially with the exposition, that before he writes another, he works out an exposition under Albrechtsberger's supervision.* Difficulties arise because Beethoven's two subjects cross at one point and so cannot be inverted properly, and the entry of one answer causes an open fourth with the end of one of the subjects. Albrechtsberger can only strike through Beethoven's work and begin afresh. The fugue is now embarked upon.† Albrechtsberger begins the exposition, but after he has fixed the third entry Beethoven gradually takes over the rest of the fugue. Albrechtsberger generally superintends the process of composition and interrupts Beethoven's work twice to give guidance. Consequently, there is no lack of *stretti* or insufficiently varied writing in parallel motion as is usually the case when Beethoven writes a fugue by himself. One wonders if Beethoven was proud of having written this fugue almost by himself because he went on to make a fair copy. Perhaps he regarded it as a model and wished merely to preserve it for reference.

Despite the difficulties which Beethoven had with double fugue, the instruction goes on to triple counterpoint and triple fugue. Albrechtsberger explains the technique with copious examples, which Beethoven summarizes. After this, they work out together‡ a draft of the various inversions of three subjects for a triple fugue, after which Beethoven writes the opening of a fugue based on them in Albrechtsberger's presence.§ The opening leap of the 1st subject is from tonic to dominant and that of the 3rd subject from dominant to tonic. Both leaps are answered incorrectly and Albrechtsberger passes them over as he did with a previous fugue (see page 22). It seems likely that this precept in writing answers was not then strictly enforced. Moreover, the matter seems to have escaped even Nottebohm's notice. Albrechtsberger corrects other points in, and adds other pieces of parallel writing to, Beethoven's opening, and helps him with various parts of the remainder of the fugue.

In another fugue,‖ Albrechtsberger writes the opening, which is then continued by Beethoven. Even now, Beethoven is still writing a number of consecutive or hidden fifths and octaves.

* *Beethoven's Studien*, p. 171.　　　　† Ibid., pp. 172 ff.
‡ Ibid., pp. 178 f.　　§ Ibid., p. 179.　　‖ Ibid., pp. 185 ff.

That he manages to introduce some inversions of the subjects to show the triple counterpoint, Nottebohm ascribes* largely to Albrechtsberger's help.

Beethoven's instruction with Albrechtsberger ends during his study of three- and four-part canon. As Nottebohm points out,* the composition of canons presents little difficulty, yet Beethoven by no means succeeded with a three-part canon written in the form of a three-part song, and Albrechtsberger has to reshape nearly half of its eight bars. Nevertheless, Beethoven goes on to write out the canon in extended form without incorporating the correction.† No wonder Albrechtsberger crossed it out! Beethoven solves two canons from Albrechtsberger's *Gründliche Anweisung zur Composition* and works two more. Then Albrechtsberger begins another,‡ perhaps for demonstration purposes, but does not continue it, and Beethoven's instruction comes to a sudden end.

In conclusion, Nottebohm pays tribute§ to Albrechtsberger's vigilance for every fault, carefulness with alterations, and constant readiness to help. He cannot be blamed for the stereotyped nature of some of his rules, nor can any great weight be attached to the fact that he was not always successful in his teaching and sometimes overlooked faults, though unevennesses in the instruction cannot be denied. Faulty teaching is found particularly in the construction of answers to fugue subjects, in which the two rules are often broken: (1) if the subject is in the tonic, the answer is in the dominant, not the subdominant, and (2) diatonic minor seconds (as from mediant to subdominant in a major key) in the subject must appear at the corresponding places in the answer. Nottebohm shows‖ that Albrechtsberger broke the rules in teaching free imitation as well, both in his own work and in his corrections of Beethoven's work, and in many of Beethoven's fugues the imitations of accompanying parts were either poor in quality or too profuse. Though Albrechtsberger taught fugue as a kind of *contrappunto fugato*, so that fugues are worked in strict counterpoint, he was not consistent in this. Some of the subjects in his collection of thirty do not lend themselves to this treatment. Even in the exercises in two-part counterpoint, a strict *cantus firmus* sometimes requires

* Ibid., p. 191.   † Ibid., p. 192.   ‡ Ibid., p. 193.
§ Ibid., pp. 193 f.   ‖ Ibid., p. 195.

a counterpoint in free style. This leads to very unsatisfactory results and made Beethoven's work more difficult and perhaps might have disgusted him.

Nottebohm speaks* of Beethoven's honest attempts in the contrapuntal exercises to master the rules and avoid faults, and the faults he made were not due to haste or carelessness. When he came on to fugue, however, he began to write hastily and made the most common mistakes that can only be attributed to carelessness and to less interest being shown. For not one fugue on two simultaneous subjects did Beethoven write a correct exposition but always needed help. The work on canon was incomplete and Nottebohm believes† there is no doubt that the instruction did not come to a natural end.

In Beethoven's works written before his lessons with Haydn which began at the end of 1792, there is scarcely any counterpoint, but predominantly figurative writing, including auxiliary notes of all kinds, arpeggio movement, runs, movement in parallel thirds, etc. When there is any contrapuntal writing in these works, it is mostly very short or incorrectly worked. References to such passages in Chapter IX demonstrate this. Beethoven's exercises in counterpoint and imitation are generally well done, and it is natural to find that he used these devices in his compositions at the time of the instruction or soon after, for example, the two-part counterpoint in the *Sonate pathétique*, Op. 13 and the Symphony No. 1 in C, Op. 21, while a comparison between the String Trios, Op. 3 (1793) and Op. 9 (1797 or 1798) shows the advance made in the confident use of imitation based on longer motifs. The same applies to double counterpoint. In works written before his instruction, mistakes can be found, but not in the works written afterwards. As regards canon, Nottebohm knows‡ of none in the style adopted by Albrechtsberger being written by Beethoven in the period immediately after the instruction. There are canons of another kind, such as Variation VII of the Fifteen Variations with Fugue, Op. 35, which show that Beethoven had appropriated the polyphonic principle.

It is a completely different matter with fugue. In this, Albrechtsberger's teaching had been so faulty that for several years Beethoven made only limited use of it. There are only the

* *Beethoven's Studien*, p. 196.   † Ibid., p. 197.   ‡ Ibid., p. 201.

26

openings of fugues, fugatos, short fugued passages, or small developments at the beginning or in the middle of a larger movement. Not until the Finale *Alla Fuga* of the Fifteen Variations with Fugue, Op. 35, do we find anything resembling a full fugue. Even then, Nottebohm asserts* that the Answer in this work is wrong, though admits that others may not agree with him. Also, he says† the Answer is wrong in the fugato of Variation VIII of the Eight Variations on *Tändeln und Scherzen* of three years earlier. Explanations of both these are offered in later chapters.

It is strange that Bach's *Das Wohltemperirte Clavier*, of which Beethoven was in his youth a notable exponent, appeared to have no influence at all on the development of his fugal writing. The real fruits of Albrechtsberger's instruction in fugue are to be found largely in the various elements of fugal writing which he taught, for example, inversions, diminutions, and *stretti*. Beethoven could henceforth use, and did in fact freely use, the fundamental parts of a fugue (such as the exposition) and fugal writing generally as an expedient in his compositions. In fact, polyphony was now admitted as a regular and effective feature of his music. When eventually he began writing extended fugues in his works, even though they reflect something of his student days, his genius had so developed that he was able to achieve far greater heights than mere mechanical technique could ever have taught him.

* Ibid., p. 197 and f.n. † Ibid., loc. cit.

III
FUGUE IN C (? *c.* 1795)

In a sketch-book in the British Museum* can be found a fugue in C for pianoforte by Beethoven which is very little known. An account of it, together with a complete transcription, was first given by A. E. F. Dickinson,† and it has since been transcribed and critically edited by Jack Werner.‡ The latter's edition however cites the fugue as 'hitherto unpublished', but it is only as a performing edition that it is published for the first time.

A comparison of the two transcriptions with each other and with the original§ is very interesting. The original is written with comparatively few alterations which suggests that the fugue had previously been sketched, though no preliminary sketches can be found. These, if any, may exist elsewhere. Beethoven must have written the fugue down in such a hurry that he has occasionally missed out a note. In his edition, Jack Werner has supplied these notes and in general has transcribed accurately. As he mentions in a prefatory note, Beethoven's handwriting is very small, and this results from exceedingly fine staves and little space between them. It is most probable that Beethoven thought little or nothing more about his fugue

* Add. MS. 29801, fo. 158.
† A. E. F. Dickinson, 'Beethoven's Early Fugal Style', *Musical Times*, Vol. 96, pp. 76 ff. (February 1955).
‡ *Beethoven: Fugue in C*, edited and arranged from the Original Autograph MS. by Jack Werner, 1956.
§ See frontispiece, to which frequent reference is made in this chapter.

once he had written the notes, for there are no dynamics, phrase-marks, time-signature, or speed indication. The fugue is clearly an early work, dating from probably not later than 1795, so that Beethoven could certainly have been expected to add a few suitable dynamics and phrase-marks. It is a great pity, however, that dynamics and other marks of interpretation occur in a large majority of the bars in Jack Werner's transcriptions and scarcely a note is free from a phrase-mark or the qualification of some nuance.

The transcription by A. E. F. Dickinson, on the other hand, reproduces Beethoven's text without any elaboration, save also for the insertion of missing notes and rests when voices are silent for a long period. Though, as this writer acknowledges, Beethoven's writing is not clear in pitch-indication, there are several incontrovertible slips in transcription. In the first part of his article, A. E. F. Dickinson gives the openings of two of the fugues (one in two parts and the other in four parts) written for Albrechtsberger, complete with the latter's corrections.* The writer gives these as two examples of, *inter alia*, 'Albrechtsberger's constant care to keep the opening tonality on the sharp or dominant side where Beethoven was too ready to let it slip flatward', and suggests that it is in this context that one should hear the fugue in C.

It is true that Albrechtsberger's corrections have this effect, but a closer examination of these passages and Nottebohm's comments† show that this was not his primary concern. In the two-part fugue in D minor Albrechtsberger makes two corrections in the opening twenty-three bars. In the first case, Beethoven's voices are a major third apart in two consecutive chords, and the correction removes the resultant tritone (or *mi contra fa*). Later in this correction a whole series of consecutive thirds by Beethoven is replaced by voices of more independent interest. At the second point Beethoven had not remembered how to dispose the second section of a fugue according to Albrechtsberger's rules, which required that the voice which begins the fugue should begin the second and third sections also. Beethoven reversed the order of entry and this gave him

---

* Op. cit., pp. 76 f. The openings of these fugues are quoted from *Beethoven's Studien*, pp. 73 and 95.

† *Beethoven's Studien*, pp. 74 and 99.

unforeseen trouble with his half *stretto*, or *semirestrictio*, so much so that instead of entering on either tonic or dominant, one voice enters on a completely different note. Albrechtsberger's subject was not guaranteed to respond to this unorthodox treatment. The correction patches up the passage as it stands, and though the first entry of the second section is made to enter on the tonic, not even Albrechtsberger can do anything really satisfactory with the second, which has to be adjusted in pitch to fit the first and is marked *Licenz*. Quite separately from this correction, Albrechtsberger demonstrates how this section should have been constructed, and the two entries of the half *stretto* are shown at the same pitch as the answer and subject respectively.

In the opening of the four-part fugue in E minor, Beethoven's mistake is a fundamental one. His first three entries are subject, answer, and answer. This is clearly against Albrechtsberger's and Marpurg's rules; there must be an alternation of subject and answer. Accordingly, Albrechtsberger resets the third entry as a subject. Since Beethoven chose for his answers the plagal, or subdominant, form given by Albrechtsberger in his list of thirty fugue themes, this substitution of a subject for the third entry necessarily involved a sharpening of the general tonality during the entry and the raising by a semitone of a note in the previous bar in preparation for the entry.

The British Museum sketch-book containing the fugue in C is a collection of 163 apparently miscellaneous loose sheets of various manufactures, mostly having little or no relation to each other, apart from some sequences of pages here and there devoted in each case to a single work. Both A. E. F. Dickinson and Jack Werner state that the sketches in this book relate to works from the Bonn period to the time of the Piano Concerto in C minor, Op. 37, which was completed by 1800; yet the sketch-book clearly begins with drafts for many of the arias and choruses from *The Ruins of Athens*, Op. 113, and *King Stephan*, Op. 117, and this is expressly confirmed in the British Museum catalogue. Both these works were composed in 1811. The fugue itself is chiefly remarkable for being the only one for the keyboard by Beethoven that is both complete and not part of a larger work, and as such, deserves a place in the Supplement to the *Gesamtausgabe*. Even so, only a cursory examination of the fugue reveals that it is not one of the master's great works and no extraordinary importance can be claimed for it in his total output!

The Fugue

Exposition

1–6*.—The Subject consists essentially of two motifs, the rhythms of which are in strong contrast:

Ex. 9

The two motifs are used extensively during the fugue, and the striding quavers of *a* resting on G form a striking foil to the neat rhythm of *b*. Both motifs have a link in that a rising third is common to each.

The Answer begins reasonably enough, with tonic harmony balanced by dominant harmony, but at $4^{1/2}$ Beethoven answers the seventh with a sixth and writes G instead of F sharp. What could and should have continued as a real Answer ending on B at 5^1 becomes a patently incorrect one, which no appeal to the practice of the great masters can justify. Beethoven knew the correct form, and the incomplete entry at 8^3 continues far enough to show this. Had he written a correct real Answer, the Subject could not have entered at 5^1, and a codetta would have been necessary. It is impossible to believe that Beethoven baulked at the effort of contriving a codetta. More probable is it that he wanted his march-like Subject to appear at regular intervals of two bars, even if a little brutality had to be shown to the latter half of the Answer.

Contrary motion is the basis of the accompaniment to the Answer. The inverted outline of *a* can be traced in the semi-quavers of 3^{1-3} and the inversion of *b* appears in $4^{2,3}$. This accompaniment does not prove to be a regular Countersubject

* The figures 1–6 mean bars one to six. Beats in a bar are indicated by superior figures. This method of numbering bars and beats is used throughout the book.

and is used only once more, and then only half of it in a varied form, in 5 (soprano).

The third entry appears in the middle part announcing the Subject. In the soprano of 6, suspensions replace the inversions of b in the bass of $4^{2,3}$, while Beethoven's handwriting in the bass of 6 is such that one cannot be certain if the notes are F, E, D, B, or F, F, E, B. Between them, A. E. F. Dickinson and Jack Werner have chosen both versions without comment, which is not surprising because in the last resort they are both possible!

Episode

7–13.—The soprano begins based on b, which is varied at 7^4, so that 7^{3-4} makes a sequential figure, heard three times, with the third statement varied. Sequence occurs in the Subject (2^{2-4}) and it is logical to find that it plays a prominent part in the fugue. Jack Werner gives E, F, E for the soprano of 7^4 but the manuscript shows clearly E, F, D. The notes of 8^4 are not so clear. Both writers give B, B, A; A. E. F. Dickinson says the second note of this beat 'looks like B but it might be C', whereas the head of the note, such as it is, is only just under the D line and strongly suggests C, giving B, C, A for the beat. This writer feels that C makes the 4th beat's answer of the 2nd beat a little laborious in view of the sequence from 7^3, whereas B (with a G understood in 9^1) makes an easy sequential phrase after 8^3. On the whole, a C seems more probable since the fugue is in an unpolished state, and this rigid repetition of 7^4 and 8^2, though it reflects the rigidity of the Subject in 2, might have been revised by Beethoven, had he worked further on the piece. The C also gives that slight hint of the dominant seventh of G that makes the progression over the barline more satisfactory.

The alto at 8^3, now more a tenor, announces most of a correct Answer, of which bass and soprano echo a at 9^1 and 9^3 to suggest a *stretto*. The bass D's (9^3-10^1) are almost certainly meant to be tied. The barline in the middle of 9 in the original was inserted in error and can be ignored. Another instance of this occurs in 16. The passage from 8^3 is partially repeated a second higher at 10^3. In his haste, Beethoven wrote the bass minim at 11^3 rather like an F, which became a distinct F for the semibreve in 12. This is obviously a slip and E, representing the dominant pedal of the current key of A minor, should be read in both cases. A. E. F. Dickinson has, however, misread the autograph in the soprano at 12², and this matter can be settled more certainly by close scrutiny than *a priori*, which method he suggests for cases where the right reading is not obvious. Beethoven's large quaver rest has been mistaken for a note, which it seems to be at first sight, but the E in 12² is written separately, and this confirms the quaver rest. The phrase from 11³ should therefore read:

Ex. 10

The soprano in 13 repeats the sequential treatment of *b* in the alto of 12, as the music modulates to the subdominant. Beethoven omitted a natural before the C in 13².

First Middle Section

14–19.—The bass opens with a complete statement of the Subject, repeated by the middle part at 16 (a flat should be understood before the B at 17¹), but the soprano entry at 18 breaks off and modulates to D minor and A minor. An F should ideally occur at 14¹ in the middle part to complete the previous phrase. The soprano of 14²/³ presents an awkward leap of a major seventh and it seems best to regard the F as the end of one phrase and the E as the beginning of the next. The dot after the F in the original is inexplicable except to render the E (14³) unnecessary.* The last note of the bar is a clear D, but this spoils the soprano line. E is preferable, and is given in both transcriptions. Since the head of the note reaches down as far as the D line (the stems of these quavers point upwards), Beethoven may really have meant C, which would have restored the chord of F. Another flat has been omitted before the B in 15². The bass in 16 is slightly reminiscent of the bass in 3,

---

* This reading was followed by Mr. Franz Reizenstein when giving the first performance of the Fugue in the B.B.C. Third Programme on 16th January 1956.

but does not attempt to recall it as a regular Countersubject. For 17^1 Jack Werner gives two quavers G, A, and A. E. F. Dickinson gives A, G. The second quaver is certainly G but has a separate tail, so that the first quaver is really a quaver rest. If $17^{1\&2}$ had consisted of four quaver notes, Beethoven would have joined them all together, which he does in every other instance.

Episode

20–25.—There is further evidence of the speed at which Beethoven wrote out this fugue and the consequent doubt about some of the notes. The last note of the alto in 21 is obviously F from the context, though it is written through the E line. More important is the course of the bass line in 23 f. From the beginning of the Episode to this point the melodic shape of *b* is always an upper or a lower mordent, and it is logical to expect mordents here. Indeed, an objective examination of the notes suggests that Beethoven wrote mordents. The only objection is the apparent tie between the 2nd and 3rd beats of 23. One is naturally loath to say Beethoven did not mean what he wrote, but it seems reasonable to suppose that in his haste he may have momentarily confused alto with soprano as the part in canon with the bass, and inserted a tie in imitation of the alto. Actually, for these four beats, the bass is in canon with the soprano at a crotchet's distance, and the rhythm of 23^3 (bass) is unmistakably the usual quaver and two semiquavers, and not the reverse as in A. E. F. Dickinson's transcription. At 24^2 there is a smudge over the bass part, but beneath it one can again still clearly see the familiar rhythm of *b* indicated, and above it, just visible, the notes B and C for the semiquavers, to provide the last of the mordents. The music of 23^1–24^3 should therefore read:

Ex. 11

The minim in the bass at 25^3 began as a crotchet A, but Beethoven later made this into a minim. Because the stave is so narrow, the minim spreads over the bottom two spaces, and A. E. F. Dickinson has mistakenly assumed that two notes are meant, C (sharp) and A. All these points Beethoven would surely have dealt with if he had revised the fugue. There are traces that the bass at 24^3 was to continue the descent, but by the end of the bar the hands would have become too wide apart to sound agreeable. Accordingly Beethoven makes the octave leap.

In this Episode sequence again characterizes the music. At 20 soprano and alto have *b* in thirds over *a* in the bass, and this is repeated a tone lower in 21. In 22 the sequence breaks up in the soprano into a two-beat figure repeated a tone higher, but the two lower parts are not strict in their sequences. The music falls again in 23, and rises in 24, governed by the soprano and alto. These sequences, alternately falling and rising, constitute a weakness in the fugue and mark it as an immature work. The unrelieved quavers in 25 seem to make a rather dull bar after so much rhythm, though they are a means of clearing the mind of the insistence of *b*, ready for the next entry of *a*.

Second Middle Section

26–27.—The bass announces the Subject in full at 26^1 and the principal feature of the other two parts is the prominent return in the soprano of the syncopation, previously only lightly hinted at in 10. To this the alto asserts crotchets on the beat.

Episode

28–32.—All three voices join in another falling sequence for two bars based on 27, leading to a chord of the diminished seventh at 30^1 and a short passage in four parts. After mentioning Beethoven's occasional use of four-part harmony where required in this fugue, A. E. F. Dickinson writes: 'Had not the master himself [Albrechtsberger] entitled his list of subjects "Themata ad *semi-restrictionem* et restrictionem apta"? Students of today will thank him for that third word.' As shown in Chapter II this Latin terminology means half *stretto* (usually at two bars' distance) and *stretto* (usually at one bar's distance) respectively, to be used in the second and third sections of a fugue, and for which treatment Albrechtsberger had specifically designed his subjects. The words do not in any way refer to the use or otherwise of an extra voice part for a few bars.

The notes in 30 in the original have undergone a certain amount of alteration, and considering its present state one could wish that Beethoven had written out the bar again more clearly. However, both transcriptions agree on a quite reasonable interpretation. For the first bass note Beethoven wrote a minim E but later wanted F. To show this he observed his frequent practice and inserted the letter f, just as he wrote *es* and *c* at 31^3 to clarify the E flat and C in the alto and tenor. In A. E. F. Dickinson's transcription the f is shown as if meaning *forte*, which would otherwise be a quite suitable dynamic indication. In the original at 32^2 a very faint dot is visible after the A minim, but A. E. F. Dickinson supplies one in brackets. At 33^1 Beethoven wrote and smudged a crotchet G for the middle part without, however, adding a crotchet rest. Jack Werner gives both note and rest, but only the note is in square brackets. A. E. F. Dickinson gives a minim rest in brackets for these two beats.

Until the end of the Episode Beethoven puts all counterpoint aside, while he makes the outside parts draw the texture together into C major and pass through the chords of very distant keys, in such a manner as he may frequently have done during one of the improvisations for which he was so famous in his youth.

Final Section

33–38.—Over a dominant pedal is heard a varied form of the Subject in the soprano, of which *a* is echoed in *stretto* by the middle part. In 34 the music again dissolves into a two-beat sequence based on *b*. After this, at 35^3, the fugue ends in four parts, with *a* prominent in soprano and tenor at 36^1, of which the alto has a variant at 36^3. After the general bustle and vigour of the fugue, thanks to the two virile motifs, it must be admitted that the conventional suspension and cadence of the last two bars is rather an anti-climax, though the soprano does recall the many mordents in 20 ff. One would not have been surprised if Beethoven had later improved 37 with references to *a* and *b*, and especially their rhythms. This is one more illustration of the rough and ready state in which the fugue was left, and lends weight to the suspicion that the manuscript was only the first draft of the composition as a whole and needed reshaping later. Why this was not done will probably never be certain.

IV

FINALE *ALLA FUGA*, FIFTEEN VARIATIONS WITH FUGUE, OP. 35
(1802)

Principal Editions:

1. *Gesamtausgabe*, XVII, 24–7 (Nr. 163), Breitkopf & Härtel, Leipzig.
2. Adolf Ruthardt, ed., *Variationen für Klavier zu 2 Händen*, I, 25–8, C. F. Peters, Leipzig.

THE Fifteen Variations with Fugue, Op. 35, have a distinctive construction. The work opens with a statement and three variations of the bass of the real theme, which serve as an introduction. This leads to the appearance of the main theme, accompanied by its bass. There then follow fifteen variations on the main theme, of which Variation VII is a canon at the octave. Variation XV is marked *Largo*, and is highly decorated, leading eventually into a final movement, which opens with the fugue. Beethoven repeats this procedure in the Thirty-three Variations on a Waltz of Diabelli, Op. 120, by preceding the double fugue (Variation XXXII) with a slow, ornate variation (XXXI). The present fugue is built on the bass of the main theme which now returns to prominence. The work ends with two further elaborate variations (not numbered) and a coda, which lead straight from the fugue and restore the supremacy of the main theme over its bass.

It has not been possible to trace any previous stylistic analysis of this work, despite its importance and its well-known connexions with other works using the same thematic material.* Only Riemann† and Tovey‡ devote more than a few words to a discussion of the fugue. Nottebohm, who has made a very thorough study§ of the sketch-book in which sketches of this work appear, informs us that sketches for the fugue, *inter alia*, are missing. This being so, it is possible to discuss only the final form of the fugue as it appears in the text of the *Gesamtausgabe*.

The Fugue

Exposition (1–16¹)

1–6¹.—The unique idea in this fugue of using the bass of the Prometheus Theme to open the Subject gives the whole work an essential architectural balance. This bass was used in the *Introduzione*, it fell into the background while the variations were elaborated, and is finally reintroduced in slightly modified form as the Subject of the Finale *Alla Fuga*. The second half of the original bass is replaced by semiquavers to obtain a sharper rhythmical contrast with the minims of the first half. The Prometheus Theme itself is also woven into the fugue, but the bass maintains its superiority and so it in no way becomes a fugue on two subjects.

So that the bass of the Theme can receive the listener's fullest attention, Beethoven prepares its entry very carefully. After the intricate elaborations of Variation XV, the beginning of the fugue is in complete contrast. Its familiarity and simplicity of construction, using only the tonic and dominant, instantly claim the attention.

The semiquavers in the Subject are not a new feature. This kind of writing appeared earlier, in the *Introduzione* (Variation

* No. 7 of the 12 *Contretänze* for Orchestra, the Ballet *Die Geschöpfe des Prometheus*, Op. 43, and the Finale of the Symphony No. 3 in E flat (*Eroica*), Op. 55.

† H. Riemann, 'Beethovens Prometheus-Musik ein Variationwerk', *Die Musik*, IX, iii. 22 (April 1910).

‡ D. F. Tovey, 'Beethoven: Fifteen Variations and Fugue "Prometheus", Op. 35', *Essays in Musical Analysis*, 1939, VI, 34. This was originally intended only as programme notes.

§ G. Nottebohm, *Ein Skizzenbuch von Beethoven*, 1865, p. 32.

a quattro), and in Variation IV, and its scalewise character is clearly seen in the opening of the second half of the Prometheus Theme. The Subject is thus related to what has gone before and unites different and contrasting elements.

6^1–11^1.—The Countersubject continues the scale movement in strong contrary motion with the Answer, a regular tonal one, which reverts to A flat on the fourth note, to effect the modulation back to the tonic key. The Countersubject is derived so completely from the Subject and follows it so perfectly that the original voice runs as an uninterrupted thought to 11^1. It is a study in motifs stated *recto* and *inverso*, a procedure exploited fully in the fugue.

The striding opening forms motif *a* (see the transcription in open score in Appendix A) and the descending seventh in semiquavers forms motif *b*, which provides subsidiary motifs *c* and *d* consisting of a third and a diminished fifth. Motif *c* has been used previously in the work, very clearly in the *Introduzione* (Variation *a quattro*):

Ex. 12

and in bars 3–4 of the canon (Variation VII):

Ex. 13

The interval covered by *d* appears in the cadential figure at the end of the first half of the bass of the Prometheus Theme:

Ex. 14

but this figure is too conventional to provide conclusive proof that it is the artistic origin of the motif.

These motifs are followed in 5 and 6 by two repetitions of *c* and one of *b*. The dissonant compass of *d* becomes an augmented fourth and is covered in four notes (*d'*). In whichever form, it plays a large part in the fugue. Motifs *c* and *d* are inverted in 7 and 8 and emptied in 9 and 10, with *c recto* and *d' inverso*. The last four quavers are a mixture of motifs. They contain an augmented inversion of *c* and a filling-in of bars 3 and 4 of *a*, softening the asperity of the augmented fourth of *d'* (inverted) in 9.

The bold, diatonic movement of the Answer contrasts with the gradual chromatic shift of the tonal centre of the alto from E flat to C and quickly back to E flat and contributes greatly to the effectiveness of the Countersubject. Moreover, the emphasis given to the D flat in 7 and 8 suggests a final cadence in A flat, so making the A flat in the Answer (9) follow naturally.

11^1–16^1.—Entry of the Subject, *forte*, in the bass. The Countersubject in the soprano is thrown up an octave to give room for the alto. The texture is kept light, and the Subject free from encumbrance. After 12, the Countersubject is transformed and hurtles scalewise through a minor ninth, an extension of *b*. With the alto accompanying in thirds, the progression of 13–14 is particularly strong. A lesser composer would probably have kept his Countersubject regular, as follows:

Ex. 15

| Bars | 11 | 12 | 13 | 14 | 15 | 16 |

The important tritone of *d'* (E flat–A natural) is retained in 14. The music modulates to B flat minor at 16, preceding which 14 and 15 can be considered as a continuous and decorated chord of the dominant seventh. This explains the otherwise surprising juxtaposition of A natural and E flat on 14^2.

The first four notes of the Subject now become more prominent and this is accentuated by the cadence at 14^1 and the apparent beginning of the Episode thereupon. The alto $(15/16^1)$ is based on *c* and is clearly taken from the *Introduzione* (Variation *a quattro*).

Episode

16^1–27.—The sequential opening incorporates the tailpiece of the Subject, which is now completely subordinated.

At 18, the tritone becomes a perfect fourth when the bass copies the soprano motifs of 14 and 16, motifs that seem to foreshadow much of the essence of the two independent Episodes in the great fugue in the finale of the Sonata in B flat, Op. 106. These motifs appear almost as an inversion of, and in *stretto* with, *b* in 18 and 19 and so reveal their importance in the Subject material.

The D in the soprano in 19 keeps the harmony complete, because the alto quits its D before the bass resolves the discord. By making the alto follow out its part logically to B flat, Beethoven also makes it more convenient for the right hand to play the important E flat (20).

This anacrusis strengthens and attracts attention to the entry in the soprano, a new treatment of familiar material. It sounds at first like a fourth voice in the Exposition because of its high register. In fact, it suggests a redundant entry of the opening of the Subject only, and is placed higher to be well separated from the bass and clearly heard. In 20–27, Beethoven, by a stroke of genius, combines the functions of redundant entry and episode.

The entry is divided between soprano and alto. Instead of going straight to E flat at 23, the alto goes to F, emphasizing the principal problem of this Subject, the unequal division of the octave into the perfect fourth and perfect fifth. In this way, Beethoven modulates to F minor, where the process is repeated in sequence. He clarifies the modulation by introducing the leading note of F minor into the theme. This use of E natural brings the tritone into the first part of the theme, and it is heard also in harmony with the soprano (22).

The entry at 20 is heard as follows:

Ex. 16

which scoring occurs at the beginning of the fugue in the finale of the Eroica Symphony, between violins and clarinets, and also between the second and first violins, bars 44–47. If the repeated quavers are considered in this revised context, their derivation from those in bar 10 of the Prometheus Theme is clearly seen. The three repeated quavers in the accompaniment to the Prometheus Theme and the three repeated B flat crotchets in bars 5 and 6 of it do incidentally show the importance of this idea and, moreover, the organic unity which Beethoven brings to his writing.

The Countersubject in the bass is regular to 21^1, as if to support the entry above it. Then it becomes a free derivation of *b*. This superficial use of the Countersubject, avoiding its rhythms, concentrates attention on the upper parts.

Middle Section

28–38^1.—In the relative minor without the normal Countersubject. The only resemblance that the staccato quavers bear to it is their stepwise movement, and they may have been inspired by the prominent quavers of 22 and 26 (soprano). The Subject, in Answer-form because it begins with a fourth, is complete and the striking dissonance at the entry (28) is made all the more effective by the upsurge of *b* (inverted) in $27/28^1$.

Again the first four notes command attention. The fourth is the predominant interval in this Middle Section so that the tonality is unfixed, and slides gradually downwards.

The semiquavers of the second part of the Subject and those of the Countersubject (regular to the beginning of 36) come more freshly to the ear after the relief from them in 28–31.

Again, as in 14–16^1, the Episode seems to start at the end of 36, before the fugue theme has finished.

43

Episode

38^1–41.—A falling sequence between soprano and alto, in a kind of double counterpoint, based on 10–12^1. Here Beethoven, with a touch of genius, adds variety to a technical procedure. Motif *b* and the motif of ascending quavers are shared alternately, but at the inversion they are displaced at a crotchet's distance. By 39^2 the soprano has stated its motif three times, in sequence, but the alto has completed only half its third statement.* It is then obliged to break off and take over *b* from the soprano, but the soprano does not wait to begin the quaver motif at the same point as the alto had done (37). It begins immediately, at the end of 39, and supplies the very notes (E natural and F), an octave higher, that would have completed the alto's third statement. Between 41 and 42 the soprano seems determined to preserve a semblance of the sequence (C, D natural, F).

Motif *b* has not hitherto received special attention. It is clearly very important in this Episode and maintains its dominance as far as 51.

Middle Section suggested

42–47^1.—Beethoven seizes another opportunity presented by the Subject, by putting the opening (42 f.) into the context of 13–14^1, where it was the third and fourth bars of the Subject. The identical notes are used, making the resemblance more striking than a transposition would have done, and suggesting a reason for returning to the key of E flat. This novel treatment of the Subject avoids using the Countersubject, and so Beethoven remodels the inversion of *d'* (cf. 14) at 43 to preserve the context of normal semiquavers and stepwise movement.

The little figure ($45/46^1$, soprano, and $46/47^1$, alto), is rhythmically based on that in the alto of $15/16^1$ and $17/18^1$, and melodically allied to the rising bass of $31^2/32^1$.

---

* One old edition of about 1850, purporting to be the 'original edition revised', gives D natural for the second quaver of 37 in the alto. D flat, understood through lack of any contradicting accidental, has the support of all other editions, and is more likely. Beethoven would not want to make the E flat chord of 37^2 so strong, nor would he have considered it necessary to strain after an exact transposition of this motif. After all, the intervals in each statement of motif *b* in the other voice are not exactly reproduced.

Episode (47¹–89)

47¹–51.—The Episode begins in a rising sequence, with *b* and the remodelled inversion of *d'*, balancing the falling sequence of the previous Episode. At 48 the alto motif is altered to avoid squareness and to merge more neatly into the exclusive use of *c* in all voices in 49–51¹. The movement of the two upper parts in thirds accentuates the reference to the *Introduzione* (Variation *a quattro*), mentioned earlier. The extended use of the diminished seventh chord (E natural, G, B flat, D flat) again emphasizes in passing the tritone and diminished fifth of *d*.

A pair of consecutive fifths occurs in 51! The ear accepts them because of the high speed and distracting entry of the soprano part.

52–65¹.—In 52 (soprano and bass), the middle note is omitted from the run of a third, which leaves nothing less than the beginning of the Prometheus Theme itself. Now displaced by a crotchet's distance, across the barline, it accompanies a new entry in the alto.* The Countersubject is again deposed in face of the powerful associations of the Prometheus Theme. Conventionally, a Middle Section is now due, but Beethoven prefers to exploit the relationship of the Prometheus Theme and its bass three times in this new rhythmical combination. Stylistic unity is preserved with familiar elements in the texture, for example, the diminished seventh from D flat to E natural (54, soprano), the tritones (53/54, bass, and 55, soprano) and *c* (55).

Each statement of the Prometheus Theme appears a tone higher than its predecessor. Had the fugue's Subject continued

---

* At 55, editions vary in giving the alto F or F sharp. It seems necessary to part company with the *Gesamtausgabe* and give F sharp. The outside parts in 54 form a diminished seventh chord. G is strongly felt to be missing in the alto. Granted an F sharp in 55, the whole chord slides down a semi-tone, is maintained until 56¹ and resolves easily on to a chord of G minor at 56². F sharps are frequent to 59 and an indisputable diminished seventh chord occurs at 60 in the corresponding place. The tritone and the fugue theme have been associated at this point before (22 and 26) and now they are associated more firmly still. If the alto at 55 is F natural, the resultant chord is the first inversion of the chord of the dominant seventh of B flat. As such, it can find no outlet in resolution. There is no doubt about the soprano A flat at 60, and there can be no real obstacle in accepting F sharp for the alto at 55.

likewise, it would have begun A–E, with the music in A minor, but the procedure is altered. In addition, the Prometheus Theme is now reinforced with the upper third, instead of the lower third. Beethoven thus achieves variety unobtrusively.

The alto of 64 follows the rhythm of 54 (soprano) and 59, but contracts the Prometheus Theme. It strikingly resembles the alto motif of 15 and 17, showing these early appearances in a new light. The contraction reduces the Prometheus Theme to a motif, handed between the two upper parts, descending harmonically in semitones.

65^2–76.—Meanwhile the bass diminishes the Subject in Answer-form to crotchets. When the parts are reversed at 69, the soprano uses the Subject, opening with the ever-present tritone. A double diminution is heard at 73, given to the soprano, the part most easily heard, so that the important change cannot fail to be noticed. A further diminution of the Prometheus Theme would spoil it, so alto and bass provide suitable harmony.

Each part has a different rhythm; the soprano has *sforzandi* on the third quaver, the syncopation in the alto causes weight on the second quaver, while the bass has a natural accent at the beginning of the bar. This conflict, together with the diminutions, breaks the music down into elements, and prepares the way for a new treatment of the material.

77–89.—The false entries of 77 and 79 give some idea of this new treatment. It is like the third species of strict counterpoint, and has been foreshadowed in 20 ff. The alto of 76/77 seems to stagnate, returning to A flat and keeping the D flat tonality. This is unnoticed in the sudden dynamic drop from *fortissimo* (valid from 62) to *piano*. 76^2 prepares for 77, and the very loud presentation of the D flat tonality is necessary to establish the tonality firmly when the dynamics change.

Only the first two notes of the Subject are important now, and they appear in two-bar sequences from 81 onwards. By 86^1 this results in a striking foreshadowing of the Answer and its final treatment in the fugue of the Sonata in A flat, Op. 110. What remains of the Subject is presented in striding common chords in a *forte* blaze. The music is reduced to two parts, in free fantasia style, displaying a more pianistic approach. In 86–89 the music works to a climax, helped by the diminution of the soprano, and the disintegration of the alto, in addition to the indication *sempre più forte*. More feeling of urgency is gained and the music prevented from sounding too thin.

Final Section, with Subject and Answer in inversion (90–132[1])

90–105[1].—The diminutions again prepare the listener for a new treatment, namely, inversion at 90 (alto), maintained into 94, with the last three notes (F, E flat, D) *recto*. Inversion of the Subject is simple, since the notes have the same names but are in different positions. The soprano (90 ff.) uses the same version of the Countersubject as in 11 ff., except that semiquavers replace the held A flat and so preserve the semiquaver movement. Motif *b* appears in a neat inverse canon between soprano and alto in 93 f.

The alto has a variation of the Countersubject, *recto* (95 ff.). In this part also, semiquavers fill up the D flat (cf. 7), but do so before reaching the D flat instead of afterwards (cf. 91). The alto of 9 and 10 is now varied by using a slow trill under C (98) and a fast trill on the D natural (99) to replace the quavers.

The regular and tonal inverted Answer is preceded by a long trill on A natural (94). This feature, originally only incidental (19), is now given prominence. The trill-anacrusis to the third entry is in the alto (99).

The Countersubject in the Exposition was more free at the third entry (11 ff.); it is also set more freely at the third inverted entry (100 ff.). Both upper parts are busy but the texture is kept clear. The soprano begins an inversion of the Counter-subject with a variation of motif *b*, and in 102/103[1] it is melodically derived from the soprano of 16–18[1]. The alto in 101 uses it and in 102 varies the alto of 15 and 17. Constant semiquaver movement is maintained. The third entry (100 ff.) exactly reproduces that in 90 ff.

105–111.—The reshaped ending of the Subject of this section is compressed in 106 ff. in the bass, so that what begins as a two-bar sequence is cleverly continued as a one-bar sequence.

Soprano and alto build a syncopated structure on this sequence from 103[1], using *c* inverted, an effect somewhat reminiscent of 49–51. The tritone and diminished fifth are outlined at various points.

The trill on C (110, bass) emphasizes the climax and leads inevitably to the thundering dominant pedal. The control of this climax from 90 is masterly. From 90 to 99 the music is *piano* in two parts, then *forte* in virtually two parts (100 f.). Writing in three simultaneous parts is established at 102. *Sforzandi*, syncopation, and sequences complete the implied *crescendo*. The reason for the thin texture in 100 f. is now apparent.

111–118.—The pedal of broken octaves is particularly apt, since it derives from the octave between the second and third notes of the Subject. Above, alto and soprano are deployed in minims and a blaze of semiquavers, from which the ear is conscious of a three-fold *stretto* (first two notes only), the pedal stopping only to allow the bass to provide the third entry (with three notes). The first two entries (112–115[1]) provide between them a suggestion of the first four notes of the inverted Subject. The now very familiar rushing scales make the *stretto* pianistically possible in 113 f.

118–132[1].—The trill (118) keeps the excitement going, while the music is poised on a single chord, as if to allow a breathing-space before the last portion of the fugue. Beethoven does not spoil the fine effect of the semiquavers by over-use, as a lesser composer might have done.

In exultation, the soprano presents a succession of rising fourths, an imitation of the opening of the Answer. Considered in pairs they suggest the contour of the first four notes of the Subject:

Ex. 17

This crotchet outline is emphasized and decorated by the scale-wise approach in semiquavers in the other part. The octave of the Subject appears in the bass in a new rhythm, *recto* and *inverso* alternately.

At 123 begin seven bars of the third inversion of the chord of the dominant seventh of E flat, the bass hammering out the A flat pedal while the octave leaps in the right hand are filled with arpeggios. A final reference to the Subject appears in 129 f., after which the music leads quietly into the Adagio.

V

FINALE, PIANOFORTE SONATA IN A, OP. 101 (1816)

Principal Editions:

1. H. Schenker and E. Ratz, eds., *Klaviersonaten*, pp. 504–7 (Vol. IV), Universal-Edition, Vienna.*
2. H. Schenker, *Die letzten fünf Sonaten von Beethoven* (*Erläuterungsausgabe*), *Op. 101*, Universal-Edition, Vienna.
3. H. Craxton and D. F. Tovey, eds., *Sonatas for Pianoforte*, III, 128–31, Associated Board of the Royal Schools of Music, London.
4. *Gesamtausgabe*, XVI, iii. 48–51 (Nr. 151).

In the composition of this sonata, there are many distinct signs of Beethoven's adoption of counterpoint as an important constituent in the texture. The first movement has traces of it, the second movement contains a canon, and the finale is thoroughly contrapuntal.

It is clear at the outset of the finale that counterpoint is to govern its style. The movement opens in double counterpoint that is so closely imitative as to suggest a canon, a style that is maintained for nearly fifty bars, when the distance between the imitating parts is widened from a crotchet to two bars. The exposition of the movement ends in a more harmonic style, the better to throw the fugal development section into

* Where editions of the sonatas vary in their bar-numbering, as with this sonata, the numbering in this edition, which is easily obtainable and the most authoritative, is used.

relief. It is natural that this development section should be in the style of a fugue in view of the contrapuntal nature of the movement. However, Beethoven does not label it as a fugue, and so allows himself some liberties of treatment. He never loses sight of the fact that this is the development section of a sonata and not an independent fugue, and he seeks to reconcile the dramatic style of the former with the intellectual style of the latter. The fugue lasts just over 100 bars, when it merges into the recapitulation, in which the imitative writing is resumed.

The Sketches

Sketches for this fugue are found in a sketch-book of 1816. Both Nottebohm* and Schenker† have studied this book and reproduced some of the sketches in their descriptions of its contents. From a collation of their reports it is possible to see something of Beethoven's train of thought in arriving at the final version.

All the sketches for this development section reproduced by these commentators are consistent with and suggest fugal treatment, and we may suppose that Beethoven never had any other intention and designed the main theme of the movement with this in mind.

The earliest sketch occurs on page 5 of the sketch-book,‡ showing the Subject already in workable form but two octaves higher than the final version and shorter:

Ex. 18

Also on page 5 is an expansion of the Subject to seven bars, at

* G. Nottebohm, 'Ein Skizzenheft aus dem Jahre 1816', *Zweite Beethoveniana*, 1887, pp. 552 ff.

† H. Schenker, *Die letzten fünf Sonaten von Beethoven (Op. 101)*, 1921, pp. 60 f.

‡ G. Nottebohm, op. cit., p. 553.

the pitch of the final version.* The decision about the pitch is thus taken early:

Ex. 19

As the square brackets indicate, Beethoven extended his Subject by developing the interval of a third, both open and filled in, inherent in the first four bars.

Apparently, Beethoven suspects monotony in the last two bars and reconstructs the Subject on page 11, thus:†

Ex. 20

Neither Nottebohm nor Schenker quotes a sketch to show any further development towards the final form of the Subject. However, speaking generally of all the sketches in this book, Nottebohm testifies‡ that the sketches gradually progress towards the ultimate shape.

Having spent the second half of the exposition of this movement in the key of E (dominant), Beethoven appears to feel that to use this key for entries in the fugal exposition, which one would expect, would provide insufficient contrast. Moreover, as the music at this point is fulfilling the function of a development section, its fugal nature would obtrude too much if tonic were answered by dominant in the customary way. This may explain Beethoven's following the style of a fugue,

* G. Nottebohm, op. cit., p. 553.
† Ibid., p. 553.   ‡ Ibid., p. 555.

with succeeding entries, but using unconventional keys for them.

At first, he uses the subdominant in the following sketch on page 5, which Nottebohm assumes* is in D major (the lack of key-signature proves nothing, as Beethoven rarely inserted one in a sketch):

Ex. 21

This version of the fugue theme is virtually the same as Ex. 18 which also shows it to be among the composer's earliest thoughts about the fugue. Schenker reproduces† this sketch, but with a few differences in the notation. It occurs, according to his pagination,‡ on leaf 3:

Ex. 22

This Schenker takes to be in D minor, modulating to A minor.

Nottebohm links§ the sketch (Ex. 21) with another on page 6 of the sketch-book, to show that Beethoven was already planning to use it in another fugato in the coda of the movement:‖

Ex. 23

---

* Ibid., p. 553 f.   † Op. cit., p. 60.

‡ Schenker uses the leaf (*Blatt*) to paginate the sketch-book, whereas Nottebohm numbers each page (*Seite*). Schenker's leaf 1 equals Nottebohm's pages 1 and 2, leaf 2 equals pages 3 and 4, and so on. Leaf 3 includes page 5 and so, failing a sight of the sketch-book, I conclude both authors refer here to the same sketch.   § Op. cit., p. 554.

‖ The parentheses and question-mark appear in Nottebohm's reproduction of the sketch and are presumably his editorial additions.

Schenker reproduces* the next stage in the effort to establish a sequence of keys. It is an extended sketch for the whole Exposition, beginning half-way through the first entry, and occurs on leaf 6. This leaf includes Nottebohm's page 11, and the sketch is possibly a continuation of the one he reproduces, despite a slight textual difference (cf. Ex. 20):

Ex. 24

My addition of a treble clef and note in square brackets shows clearly that Beethoven answered A minor by C major, returned to A minor for the third entry, and ended with C major for the fourth. C major is just as directly related to A minor as dominant is to tonic. In an unconventional way, Beethoven has approached his problem quite logically. This, then, is an important stage in the composition of the fugal exposition.

* Op cit., p. 60.

This idea is not finally adhered to, for, on the front side of leaf 7* appear two sketches, in D minor and A minor respectively, in which Beethoven is working out a Countersubject:†

Ex. 25(a)

Ex. 25(b)

On the back of this leaf‡ are the following sketches, reproduced by Schenker.§ The former shows a rather ordinary accompaniment to an entry in D minor. The latter, however, shows the Countersubject drawing in part on the eventual form of the second half of the Subject (quavers) and in part on an imitation of the Subject, similar to the style of the exposition of the movement. It is the first hint of the final form of the Countersubject. Even at this stage, the Subject is not in its finished state.

Neither Nottebohm nor Schenker reproduces any more sketches showing further development in the material of the

Ex. 26

---

* 'Blatt 7 (Vds.)', i.e., page 13. Schenker differentiates between the sides of a leaf by adding *Vorderseite* (Vds.) or *Rückseite* (Rücks.).

† H. Schenker, op. cit., p. 60.

‡ 'Rückseite des Blattes 7', i.e., page 14.   § Op. cit., p. 60.

Ex. 27

Exposition. However, they quote between them sketches for other parts of the fugue which are instructive.

According to Schenker,* final improvements occur from leaf 7, 149 ff. are worked out on leaf 10† with 149 and 151 in their final form, and the redundant entry at 155 is fixed, even to the displacement of the accent. Great progress is shown on the back of leaf 12 and the front of leaf 13,‡ where 152–155 are sketched:

Ex. 28

159/160–167 are sketched on the same page in a much more extended form:§

Ex. 29

---

* Op. cit., p. 60.   † 'Blatt 10'.
‡ 'Blätter 12 (Rücks.) und 13 (Vds.)', i.e., pages 25 and 26.
§ H. Schenker, op. cit., p. 61.

A little later, though Schenker does not say* exactly where, occurs this draft of 182 ff.:

Ex. 30

Quite early in the sketch-book, Beethoven worked at the possibility of a *stretto*. Schenker quotes† this from the front of leaf 4:‡

Ex. 31

On the back of this leaf,§ occurs this sketch which Schenker believes‖ is a preliminary to the final dominant pedal, but which seems to bear little resemblance to this section of the fugue, apart from being written in sixths:

Ex. 32

* Ibid., loc. cit.   † Ibid., p. 61.   ‡ 'Blatt 4 (Vds.)', i.e., page 7.
§ 'Blatt 4 (Rücks.)', i.e., page 8.   ‖ Op. cit., loc cit.

Both Nottebohm* and Schenker† reproduce an extended sketch for the final section of the fugue from 208[2]:

Ex. 33

E moll

The only other sketch quoted is by Schenker,‡ who reproduces an example of augmentation from the back of leaf 3:§

Ex. 34

8 con B.

It is noteworthy that Beethoven was really augmenting his first

* Op. cit., p. 554. Nottebohm says the sketch is on page 27.

† Op. cit., p. 61. Schenker places the sketch on 'Blatt 14 (Vds. und Rücks.)', i.e., pages 27 and 28.

‡ Ibid., p. 61.

§ 'Blatt 3 (Rücks.)', i.e., page 6.

sketch for the opening bars of the movement, which ran as follow:*

Ex. 35

Letzte presto

The double augmentation of the semiquavers points to the use of double augmentation at the end of the fugue, which Beethoven may have been trying out here, even though the sketch comes near the beginning of those for the fugue. This early sketch may also have prompted Beethoven to use an entry in the subdominant in his fugal exposition.

Schenker mentions† other augmentations (without reproducing them) to be found on the front of leaf 7‡ and both sides of leaf 8,§ where they appear already in combination with the low E in bars 223 ff. at the end of the fugue.

Before examining the fugue as it is, it is interesting to consider a reconstruction of the Exposition as it might have been if tonic had been answered by the conventional dominant. In this, I have tried to adhere to Beethoven's style of composition as much as possible, in order to focus attention on the differences arising from his unusual key-order of entries. This

* G. Nottebohm, 'Ein Skizzenbuch aus den Jahren 1815 und 1816', *Zweite Beethoveniana*, p. 343.

† Op. cit., p. 61.

‡ 'Blatt 7 (Vds.)', i.e., page 13.

§ 'Blatt 8 (Vds. und Rücks.)', i.e., pages 15 and 16.

59

reconstruction should be considered not only as the beginning of a fugue, but also as the start of the development section of the whole movement, which was Beethoven's intention (see Ex. 36).

If the fugue had been worked out with such an Exposition, the listener would have had the impression of two very distinct styles being used, the sonata style and the fugal style, so familiar is the answer of tonic by dominant and vice versa in a fugue. The second half of the Subject clearly asserts a downward movement: A, G, F, E, which is repeated in the first half of the Answer, with the disturbing exception of the F sharp. This covering of the same ground twice occurs with each entry, and tends to give a cumulative effect of monotony. The nearness of the F sharps in the second and fourth entries to the F naturals

Ex. 36

(Geschwind, doch nicht zu sehr, und mit Entschlossenheit.)

in the previous entries distracts a little from that unity of effort needed at the opening of a fugue.

If this reconstruction is compared with Beethoven's Exposition it will be seen that, though Beethoven's key-order is unusual, each entry follows naturally on its predecessor. Schenker was aware of this in his analysis.* He draws attention to the essential shape of the Subject as a continuous descent. This for a subject in the minor scale means the melodic form. Being in A minor, the Subject at this point uses therefore only the white notes of the pianoforte, and leads naturally to an entry in C major. The strong use of B flat begun in the Countersubject means that the Answer is modified into the descending form of D melodic minor, the key of the next entry. Both the B flat

* Op. cit., p. 58.

and the C sharp become naturalized, enabling the tonality to revert to A minor for the fourth entry. Considered thus, the Exposition leaves no doubt that the Subject is in A minor (the tonic minor of the key of the movement) and not in C major, as Nagel assumes.*

The Fugue

Exposition (123^2–160^2)

123^2–130^2.—The Subject is cleverly constructed and is ideally suited for fugal use. Its strongly contrasting rhythms are very characteristic of many of Bach's subjects. The juxtaposition of a held crotchet and semiquavers in 124 and 126 calls naturally for imitation at a half-bar's distance. Three motifs comprise the material of the Subject:

Ex. 37

Motif *a*, a plain drop of a third, is followed by *b* of rising semiquavers and a drop of a fifth. Together, they are the minor version of the opening exposition of this movement (32^2–34^1). Now, however, the two motifs are preserved in exact tonal sequence so that the tonic can be the bottom note of the Subject at 127 (cf. G sharp at 36). The longer *c* in sturdy staccato quavers is also repeated in sequence. The octave leap in 127 provides a fine opportunity to divide the Subject into two halves, which are in marked contrast with each other, yet are balanced by their descending nature and emphasis on the interval of a third as the upper square brackets show. Though the two semiquavers in 130 are not part of the Subject, they make another third with the end of it. It is not fanciful to detect

* W. Nagel, *Beethoven und seine Klaviersonaten*, 2nd edn. (1924), II, 240 f. Nagel makes corresponding errors in giving the keys of later entries.

another unifying influence between the two halves of the Subject. The outline of the first half (C, B, B, A) perhaps suggested the repeated notes in the second half.

130^2–137^2.—While the Answer is being heard, the bass continues with the Countersubject in the rhythmical manner of 32^2–36, but the semiquavers are now in contrary motion, so that superficially the Countersubject inverts *b*. To have preserved the almost canonical style of the former passage as a *stretto* would have been out of place so early in the fugue. Also, too close a similarity with the original manner would spoil the fugue as a development section. Even so, Beethoven manages to introduce a hint of canon on *c*, at a bar's distance, from 134. The tenor's Answer continues the motif and gives the effect of canonical writing as far as 137^2.

137^2–145^2.—Though the texture of the fugue appears closely knit, Beethoven's style is not always absolutely strict. Where necessary the claims of fugue give way to the overriding claims of sonata. So here, at the third entry, the Countersubject is placed a third lower than one would expect. The bass accompanies this in thirds, and while this incidentally emphasizes the importance of the thirds, already noted, Beethoven was here following a practice advocated by Fux and Albrechtsberger.* The lowering of the Countersubject means that it does not always fit with the fugue theme; an adjustment has to be made in 139. The tenor moves to a G instead of A, but resumes A in 140. The little canon appears again (141–144) between alto and bass. The tenor (142) does not play E, E, D in sixths with the bass, as seems natural. With what object Beethoven wrote the three D's in his autograph for preference is not clear. Certainly he avoids a $\frac{6}{4}$ chord on the second quaver but, as this carries no accent, its use would have caused no aural offence. $\frac{6}{4}$ chords are used in this way in 144, 150, and 152. The alto's codetta in 145 carries on the thought of the fugue theme excellently, stressing the third in its sequential fall:

Ex. 38

* See Chapter II.

145^2–155^1.—The original key of the Subject returns for the fourth entry and the Countersubject in the alto begins at the same distance from the Subject as was the bass at 131 ff., and accompanied in sixths by the tenor. The Countersubject is broken off at 148^2 and is resumed by the tenor at 150^1, while the alto takes over the accompaniment in sixths.

At first sight, the harmony seems odd in 146. Heard in performance, the music moves so quickly that the A minor tonality is felt continuously through the bar. The semiquavers do not conflict with that tonality but decorate it and in 147 they decorate the resolution. An inspection of the Subject shows that the semiquavers perform the same function there. They clothe the bare outline of the Subject with the lively b, leaving the Subject basically simple, but impelling the music along.

The canon is again present at the end of the entry (149–152) and each part pursues its way resolutely at the expense of the resultant harmony. At 152^2 soprano and alto even produce a pair of consecutive fifths, but they are scarcely audible at high speed.

A short codetta of two bars follows (152^2–155^1), continuing in a descending style, but the soprano line is now made syncopated by tying the repeated notes.

155^1–160^2.—A redundant and compressed entry of the fugue theme in the key of the second entry appears in the bass, displaced by a crotchet's distance. Against this, the Countersubject in the soprano is introduced by a fall and a rise of a third in 155^1 which further stress the special treatment this interval receives in the fugue. This bass entry is modified in various ways to suit the other parts and to allow the music to move to the Episode. In 157^1 Beethoven writes G, instead of F, to fit the upper parts. In 160 the last bar of the Subject has a slightly amended rhythm to avoid consecutive ninths with the soprano. This entry has two elisions: the last bar but one of the Subject is elided completely and also two quavers in 159. In this bar the Countersubject is transferred from the soprano to the alto which also, in 160, compresses into one bar the material of two. Meanwhile, the soprano imitates at a half-bar's distance what is left of c in the bass.

Episode

160^2–172^2.—The soprano, accompanied in similar motion by alto and bass (161 f.), continues with *c*, and neatly dovetails the Episode on to the end of the Exposition.

Each statement of the motif now incorporates the two semiquavers originally attached to the end of the Subject in 130, which lightens the procession of quavers. While the motif appears in the inner parts (163 f.) and later (165 f.) in all three upper parts, the bass, nominally a free part, follows the outline of the fugue theme (161–165). In 167, the semiquavers appear more frequently in order to lead into another part of the Episode based on *a* and *b*, though the initial quaver of *a* is mostly absent. The fifths which end *b* are too final for an Episode and many are changed to the less definite thirds. The texture is very low, but is saved from being muddy by plenty of rests and only one part sounding semiquavers at once. On Beethoven's thinner-toned pianoforte it would have sounded less muddy still.

Middle Section

172^2–182^1.—By dropping through a third (169–173), the bass guides the harmony easily to the relative major key for an entry in C major (172^2 ff.). As is usual in a development section of a sonata movement, there is constant modification of existing material, and here the Subject is varied. The idea of ending *b* with a third instead of a fifth has been a feature of the Countersubject and became more noticeable in 155 ff. when the Countersubject appeared in the soprano, and more marked still in the Episode (169 ff.). It now influences the form of the Subject at 175/176, when it goes to E instead of C. The rhythm of the Subject is followed and preserves the feeling of an entry. Moreover, the different shape prevents any feeling that this is part of a counter-exposition. This change at 176 establishes the key of C major more completely, which is the purpose of this entry. The Countersubject in the tenor supports this by omitting the B flats and the bass reinforces the key with a gentle variation of *b* down to the tonic.

The Countersubject also breaks off at 176^2 to accompany the alto in tenths, and the canonical idea is maintained by the bass. At 179 the harmony sounds strained, but the second C in the bass is simply an appoggiatura resolving to B. The doubled major third here would offend the strict, conventional musician, but it serves to emphasize the importance of the third, even harmonically, and shows how much Beethoven needed imitation in this fugue. After a short codetta (179^2–182^1) the Episode begins.

Episode (182^1–208^2)

182^1–193^2.—Having carried on thus far in a manifestly fugal style, Beethoven finds that it is time now to adopt a freer style if the fugal manner of this Development section is not to make it outweigh the rest of the movement. Accordingly, he adjusts the balance between the sonata and fugal styles with a more pianistic section for nearly thirty bars until another entry appears (208^2). In this very long Episode, Beethoven merges *a* and *b* into a single motif which may well be called *ab'* since the final interval is variously replaced.

Now, for the first time, the direction of the music is upward. As far as 196^1, the whole structure is gradually lifted up by the bass which turns itself into the tenor part. The small drops at the end of *ab'* help this rise. The motif is further contracted to a bar in length, with no held note in it, and is exchanged between the parts sequentially. Beethoven writes G instead of F in the alto of 185^1 (cf. 158, bass), though nothing is gained by this. F is essential to the chord of the dominant seventh here. Indeed he uses F in 187^1 (bass). Other surprising notes are the tenor's D (186^1) and E (188^1).

After four bars (182–185) the structure is inverted, and the ends of the motif (now in tenor and bass) are freer still. The accompanying parts leap octaves inspired, possibly, by the leap in 127. It is a moot point whether Beethoven was seeking to introduce the B, A, C, H idea, albeit transposed, in the outline of the soprano here:

Ex. 39

The B, A, C, H motif did interest Beethoven and we know that he projected an overture on it between 1822 and 1825.* In addition, he studied Bach's fugues for some years before writing this and the other 'late' sonatas in which fugal writing becomes so much more important. Beethoven made some sketches for a quintet as a memorial to Bach in 1809, though not on the B, A, C, H theme.†

From 190 the motif gradually disintegrates until at 193 it is broken up. Soprano and alto combine in a chromatic descent, again through a third, of which the only foreshadowing is in the alto of $154-155^1$. The contrary motion here is a strong feature in enabling the listener to accept the chromaticism. The spacing of Beethoven's texture in these bars is remarkable for its clarity.

193^2-208^2.—The semiquavers of b now become the basis for the rushing scale passages of the next section of this Episode. Here too, the tonality of the dominant key, deliberately omitted from the Exposition, appears for the first time. A fully pianistic style emerges, so far removed from normal fugal style that it is difficult to trace the four voices. Contrapuntal implications are reduced to a minimum with constant parallel movement in thirds, sixths, and tenths. Four bars in E minor (194–197) are followed in sequence by another four in the relative major, G (198–201), a progression that once more emphasizes the third.

At 201, the soprano is given a very varied and contracted form of the fugue theme rhythmically displaced by a half-bar; this has been prepared for by the *sforzandi* in 194 and 198. The repeated notes of c are now tied (204–206), an idea which was first used in 153–154 (soprano). The first part of the theme is accompanied by the tenor in tenths while alto and bass, also in tenths, dovetail a suggestion of the Countersubject. This manner of composition, based on the teachings of Fux and Albrechtsberger, has already been well prepared in the Exposition and from 194. Canonic interest is again maintained with the four-fold entry of the syncopated variation of c at 204^2 ff., while the bass and alto run scalewise through

* G. Nottebohm, 'Liegengebliebene Arbeiten', *Zweite Beethoveniana*, pp. 577 ff.

† G. Nottebohm, 'Skizzen aus dem Jahre 1809', *Zweite Beethoveniana*, pp. 268 f.

over four octaves in semiquavers.* This four-fold entry fore-shadows the final section, with an effect of *stretto maestrale*.

Final Section (208^2–231)

208^2–223^1.—The *stretto* is introduced in the same order of voices as the Exposition, i.e., from bass to soprano. After giving only *a* and *b* the bass holds a dominant pedal, another indication of the close of the fugue and of the final pedal at 223^2. The alto entry is cut short at the end of 210 but the soprano gives it *a* for another and complete entry while efficiently giving its own entry as well, accompanied by the tenor. In all, the effect is of a five-voiced *stretto*, which heightens the tension, and recalls powerfully the fugal nature of this Development section.   The final note, G sharp (212, soprano) is made a quaver so that the alto can be heard giving the motif again. From 210^2 to 214^1 the alto is in another *stretto* with the soprano and tenor for the first half of the fugue theme, also at a half-bar's distance, so that *stretto* is maintained for six bars.

From 214^2, the second half of the fugue theme (*c*) is also treated in close imitation, and in the tonic key of the fugue, A minor. This motif has lent itself to canonical treatment before in the fugue, but never with all four parts. However, this is virtually two-part writing, because the soprano and tenor accompany in sixths, which later become thirds. The end of the fugue is clearly in sight as the motif is clipped to the first three quavers (218 ff.). A drop of an octave (220/221) in the lower parts enables the music to rise to the dominant pedal and the climax of the fugue. To impel the music towards the climax the soprano, followed by the alto, reintroduces the semiquavers attached to the end of the Subject (cf. 160–167).

223^2–231.—Immediately after the climax in 223, Beethoven gives a double augmentation of *a* and *b* in the bass, over a low E pedal, marked by him 'Contra E', to remove any doubt about the use of a then exceptionally low note. The highly dramatic chord of the diminished seventh prevails until the resolution in 227. Upper parts are based on *b* and *c*.

The parts and indeed, the fugue, completely disintegrate

---

* In the soprano of 204, the two A's are clearly tied in Beethoven's manuscript, but the tie is omitted in the Original Edition, the *Gesamtausgabe*, and by Tovey.

into arpeggios on the dominant chord at 228. Beethoven's specific use of the sustaining pedal enables him to have this chord sounding throughout the entire range of the keyboard, heralding the recapitulation in a mounting climax of joy.

VI

FINALE, PIANOFORTE SONATA IN B FLAT, OP. 106 (1818–19)

Principal Editions:

1. *Klaviersonaten*, pp. 541–56 (Vol. IV).
2. F. Busoni, ed., 'Analytische Darstellung der Fuge aus Beethoven's Sonate, Op. 106', *Johann Sebastian Bach: Klavierwerke*, I (*Das wohltemperierte Klavier*, Book I), 195–205, Breitkopf & Härtel, Leipzig.
3. *Sonatas for Pianoforte*, III, 175–90.
4. *Gesamtausgabe*, XVI, iii. 83–96 (Nr. 152).

THIS fugue is virtually the whole of the finale of what, in many respects, is the greatest of all pianoforte sonatas. In the earlier movements there are examples of contrapuntal writing, but nothing so extraordinary as to presage this final movement. There is a short fugato in the first movement, beginning at 137, and arpeggios in canonical style in 54 ff. of the Scherzo. The introduction to the fugue, which acts as a transition from the slow movement, contains some short passages of imitation. The fugue arises naturally from this introduction, without a break. It continues its headlong course for nearly 400 bars, with only a bar's rest and a tranquil section of unearthly beauty of twenty-nine bars just over half-way through for respite.

Of particular interest is the opening leap of a tenth. This leap (or sometimes a third) occurs in the first bars of all four movements of the sonata, and in the first movement the affinity is very striking. Each of the other three movements and the introduction to the fugue use the third considerably, and so now does the fugue. In this way Beethoven preserves the thematic kinship between the movements, of which Marion Scott writes.*

During the course of the fugue, Beethoven shows an unerring command of almost every kind of technical device, yet devises a work of great art, which must surely silence all those critics who doubt his power to write a fugue.

The Sketches

Nottebohm quotes† four sketches for the Subject of this fugue:

Ex. 40

The characteristics common to all of them are the initial leap of a tenth and the contour of the opening: F–A–B flat–G–E flat. It is possible, though Nottebohm does not say, that they are in the order of composition. The first sketch is somewhat solid and inflexible because of its two opening minims. Had the F been an octave higher, the rigidity would not have been so apparent, but Beethoven wants the big leap particularly, to arrest attention for all the many appearances of this Subject

* M. M. Scott, *Beethoven*, 4th edn. (1943), p. 145.

† G. Nottebohm, 'Skizzen zur Sonate, Op. 106', *Zweite Beethoveniana*, p. 136.

in the fugue. He seems in this sketch to be more concerned with how the Subject should begin than how it should continue, but the *etc.*★ suggests that it was meant not only to continue, but probably also in the same style, namely, quavers. Beethoven follows this procedure in all the other sketches to a greater or less degree, and also in the final version.

The F is shortened to a crotchet in the second sketch, and the leap becomes much more distinctive. The Subject is now sketched in the triple time that results from this revision. This leads to a series of triplets in bars 3, 4, and 5 of the second sketch, which foreshadow the semiquavers of the final version. The second sketch sounds unsatisfactory because marked rhythm is abandoned too soon and each triplet of bar 5 begins on D. The Subject still seems too ordinary.

In the third sketch Beethoven reverts to the former bar lengths. The trill is now introduced, but it is difficult, especially when one knows the final form of the Subject, to see the object of anticipating the note of the trill. The force of the trill is weakened and the striking rhythm is nullified. Possibly Beethoven was trying to avoid the squareness of the first sketch, this time in crotchets. Now he has gone to the other extreme of ornateness. The third sketch is the most rhythmical, but too monotonously so for a full-length fugue. Between bars 2 and 3 it stagnates a little, though the similar stagnation between bars 4 and 5 suggests it was deliberate.

The fourth sketch shows a marked advance on the others. The first three bars are almost in their final version with triple time firmly established. Though now virtually satisfied about how the Subject should start, Beethoven must have been dissatisfied with its length of little more than four bars, and have sought to expand it to the six bars used in the second and third sketches, and implied by the *etc.* of the first. The opening three notes of the Subject range over an eleventh. Beethoven seems now to be fully aware that this contains five steps of a third, the interval which is so important. This sketch is the only one to exploit the fact fully. The final crotchet of the rhythm:

★ It is explained at the end of the *Einleitung* to the *Zweite Beethoveniana* (p. X) that 'etc.' is always Beethoven's own marking and 'u.s.w.' (*und so weiter* = and so on) shows Nottebohm's abbreviation. To prevent confusion, I have retained the original 'etc.' and 'u.s.w.' on all occasions.

♩ ♫ ♬ | ♩ is changed into semiquavers which generate more semiquavers and give the outline of the five falling thirds, which I have asterisked. The drops occur at first after every three crotchets and then after every crotchet. This sudden trebling of the rate of the fall is unnatural and too precipitate.

The defect is remedied in the final version by giving the rhythm: ♩ ♫ ♬ | ♩ twice in full, which on the one hand justifies its existence, and on the other delays the next fall of a third by a further crotchet. The falls are now more evenly graduated and come successively after 3, 3, 2, 1, and 1 crotchets instead of after 3, 3, 1, 1, and 1 crotchets, as in the fourth sketch. So near did the fourth sketch prove to be to Beethoven's final version that he could also preserve intact the passage marked ┌────┐.

The Fugue

Exposition (16–40)

16–25.—It is clear from the sketches how determined Beethoven was on making the third the chief interval in the outline of the Subject. These thirds, marked here ┌────────┐, can be clearly seen:

Ex. 41

Though Nagel[*] holds that the Subject is only five bars long, Busoni[†] and Tovey[‡] have a stronger case in reckoning it as

---

[*] W. Nagel, *Beethoven und seine Klaviersonaten*, 2nd edn. (1924), II, 297.
[†] F. Busoni, ed., *Johann Sebastian Bach: Klavierwerke*, I, 195.
[‡] D. F. Tovey, *A Companion to Beethoven's Pianoforte Sonatas*, 1931, p. 244.

six bars long, especially as Beethoven uses six bars in the *cancrizans* presentation of the Subject at 153 ff.

In analysing the Subject into motifs, it is impossible to agree entirely with either Busoni or Tovey; they are, however, essentially correct in their dissections. Beethoven hints at the opening of the Subject in the bass at the beginning of the *Allegro risoluto* (11). This opening of three notes forms *a* ($16–17^1$). Its rhythm has been given further force by making the F only a quaver, compared with the crotchet of the fourth sketch, though it is very likely that Beethoven thought of it as being staccato. This staccato effect throws extra emphasis on the A and makes the trill more exciting. As Edwin Hall Pierce shows,[*] this trill is by no means ornamental, but structural in a high degree. The dominant harmony of 16 leads triumphantly to the tonic. The two downward scale passages of *b* move strongly to G and E flat respectively; it too has been suggested in the right hand of the *Allegro risoluto* (14 and 15). A third statement of *b* begins in 19 but breaks up the scale and becomes a new motif, *c*, hinted at in the *Allegro risoluto* (16), right hand, as the Subject enters. Having reached the original note of the Subject, Beethoven continues the semiquavers in a new, rising motif, *d*, repeated sequentially in 21. This uses an inverted turn, as opposed to the normal turns of *c*.

The Answer is delayed by an extensive codetta of four bars, in which 20 and most of 21 are repeated in 22 and 23. A lesser composer would have avoided this repetition as contrary to the nature of a fugue and introduced his Answer at 22. Such a composer would scarcely have contrived this Subject in the first place! The melodic level is pushed higher but never as far as the B flat of 17. From 24 the level drops in a series of inverted turns, continuing to do so in 26 as the Answer enters.

26–34.—Beethoven begins his Answer correctly with B flat, and the interval is consequently widened to an augmented eleventh. With characteristic thoroughness he has prepared the listener for this entry in 21 and 23, where the same two notes are given the identical rhythmical effect by being in the same positions in the bar.

* 'The Significance of the "Trill", as found in Beethoven's most mature works', *Musical Quarterly*, XV, 241 f. (April 1929).

The first Countersubject proper begins at 27[1]:

Ex. 42

Its first rhythm (*e*) suggests a diminution of *a*. Here, as in 16, F and A are juxtaposed, this time between the two voices. The new motif is expanded into *e'* in 29, and *f* in 30–32[1] is allied to it. In the succeeding codetta, the alto repeats the opening of *f*, while the soprano develops the inverted turn of *d* more freely than before. For all this ornamentation the resultant harmony is quite simple. The turn is not of course purely ornamental; it is the means of imparting relentless energy and drive to the fugue, without complicating the harmonic texture.

35–40.—Now that the two upper parts have been driven high, Beethoven can give the bass the Subject, over which the soprano has the first Countersubject. The alto has what proves to be a second, rather subsidiary, Countersubject for four bars and then becomes the same as the first Countersubject in 40:

Ex. 43

It begins with *g*, rhythmically imitative of the first Countersubject, and a distinctive figure (*h*) follows in 39.

Episode

41–51[3].—The two upper parts alternate *h* and the beginning of *f*, while the bass continues the surging semiquavers which are an almost constant feature of the fugue. These semiquavers are a free mixture of *c* and *d*. Arpeggios help the bass to maintain some contact with the other two parts, as the whole structure rises to 44. From 45[3] *f* and *h* become diminished and fragmentary in the soprano and alto and these parts recede in importance and strictness to make way for the reappearance of *a* in 47 after a lapse of nearly thirteen bars.★

★ In the bass of 45[3], there is no accidental in front of the second semi-quaver in the Original Edition so that E flat is to be understood. Ratz adds

Alto and bass alternate this motif every bar. It is now advanced by a crotchet from its original position in the bar. This gives a still greater accent to the minim and makes a variation on the original version. The first statement begins on B flat as did the Answer and seems to require to go to E natural. The Subject form then replies in 48/49. Thereafter the leap is kept at a tenth. Meanwhile the soprano takes over the semiquavers. These are very free and have only an odd reference to c and d. All attention is now focused on the lower parts, of which the alto is strengthened by diminished sevenths, a dramatic interval in those days, with the soprano at 48^1 and 50^1. As long as the soprano is still cognate in some respect with what has preceded, then the mind accepts it without attending to it.

First Middle Section with Subject rhythmically displaced (51^3–71^1)

51^3–57^2.—The alternation of a ends. Instead of the alto stating it in its turn, it is left in the bass. This necessitates rewriting the opening rhythm which seems now to take a hint from e (27), by eliminating the quaver rest. The Subject follows in full in D flat. Here possibly is one of the licences Beethoven mentions.* No ordinary composer would have had his first Middle Section in such a remote key and unaccompanied by the Countersubject. What Beethoven does is not so unrelated to the Exposition as it seems at first. In 51^3/52 the alto accompanies the Subject in a way that recalls 16. A comparison of this reconstruction of 51^3–56^1 using the Countersubjects, with Beethoven's version, shows that his harmonies are essentially the same:

Ex. 44

Bars   51   52   53

the flat but says that later editions insert a natural and assume that E natural is intended. Busoni, Tovey, and the *Gesamtausgabe* have E natural. As the music is in D minor at this moment, E natural seems more logical.

* He writes *Fuga a tre voci, con alcune licenze* at the head of this fugue.

As in his other fugues, the parallel tenths between bass and soprano enrich the texture without complicating it. The alto adds a little chromatic motif which is related to the chromaticisms in the Subject (20 f.). At 55^2 it becomes the end of e' and f, which the soprano accompanies* in 56 f.

57^3–65^1.—A codetta of episodic proportions follows. The alto and bass of 55^3–57^2 are apparently inverted by the soprano and bass from 57^3, but the soprano starts a crotchet too soon. This is ingeniously rectified by the addition of four semiquavers in 58^2, soprano, which then gives that part two complete statements of the sixth bar of the Subject. Meanwhile, the alto reproduces the former soprano part. In both 57 and 59 it is the part furthest from the semiquavers that gives way to avoid the stretch of a tenth. This preserves the double counterpoint in two adjacent parts. The repetition caused by this inversion seems to balance and justify that at 22 and 23.

From 59^3 soprano and bass alternate the opening of f, a succession which resembles the alto of 32–34, but this time advanced rhythmically by a crotchet. The bass octaves increase the sonority. The inverted turn of d returns to prominence in the alto. From 63^3, f again becomes diminished and fragmentary and recedes from the argument (cf. 45^3–47^2), to prepare for the Answer in the soprano.

65^2–71^1.—Motif a is kept shortened as at 51^3, but the theme is again displaced, now delayed by a crotchet (or, if one prefers, advanced by a further crotchet). The Answer is set at an

* In the soprano of 57^2 the flat is missing before the G in the Original Edition and several editions assume G natural is intended. Ratz says that a certain decision is scarcely possible, but in spite of the key-signature the music has definitely been in the key of D flat from 52^3 and does not soon quit it after the point in question. All G naturals occurring in these bars are chromatic. As this note is part of a straightforward diatonic scale, G flat seems therefore the more probable reading. Both Busoni, Tovey, and the *Gesamtausgabe* give G flat.

unprecedented height, and logically so, after the great increase of excitement from 59. Below the Answer, the two lower parts are ingeniously crossing their parts, allowing for octave transpositions, as follows:

Ex. 45

To have done this exactly, Beethoven should have written F in the alto at *, but he had made his point by this time. The texture of 69^2–71^1 is an inversion of 55^3–57^2 and consequently the bass at 70 begins to accompany the alto in thirds, but reverts to sixths in 71.

Episode

71^2–84.—Beethoven begins by inverting 69^2–71^1 with modifications. When the bass takes over the semiquavers at 71^2 it joins perfectly with the soprano and continues to reproduce the first two bars of the original codetta (cf. 22 f.). A six-fold imitation of 72^2–73^1 follows until 79^1. A slight alteration is made in 73^2 to give a diatonic scale, both up and down; Beethoven finds it a good figure for using in double counterpoint with the second bar of *f* in these six imitations.

In the bass of 79^3/80^1 Beethoven fills his leap of a tenth by an arpeggio and disguises an entry of *a*, against which almost all *f* is fitted. A suggestion of its repetition in sequence comes in 81^3–83^2. The bass of 83^3 f. freely imitates the soprano's *f* as the music modulates to G flat.

Independent Episode

85–93.—Apparently new material is introduced, but it is not entirely new as Tovey categorically asserts* and Busoni implies.† It would be inartistic to do so once a movement had got under way. Ideas that seem new in great works are often

★ Op. cit., p. 246.   † Op. cit., I, 197.

related to what has preceded. Here the soprano begins with an obvious variation of the leap of a tenth in *a*. The bass of $79^3/80^1$ showed Beethoven using the arpeggio to fill it in; now he fills in the top third and casts it in a different rhythm. The resultant motif:

Ex. 46

is therefore best labelled *a'*. Similarly, Beethoven derives the alto motif from the soprano of $83–84^1$, as follows:

Ex. 47

This then can be labelled *f'*.

The bass run in 85 occurs occasionally and is chiefly used to complete the harmony. It is too short to be capable of indisputable derivation; nevertheless it is rhythmically in keeping with *a'* and *f'* and with the rest of the fugue. These motifs are heard regularly in each part to 92. Frequently, Beethoven prefixes *a'* with a solitary semiquaver, which resembles 85^1, where the D flat belongs musically to the close of the previous section. In the alto of 87^1 the F helps to stabilize the rhythm, and in 90^1 it completes the harmony. Pianistic considerations raise the opening of *a'* by an octave in the bass at 88^1 and 91^1. On the last beat of the same bars this opening is omitted in the soprano to avoid crossing with the alto, which extends the opening of *f'* into a downward scale. Fragments of this motif lead, in the soprano of 93, to a high point and a Middle Section in E flat minor in augmentation (94).

Second Middle Section in Augmentation $(94–116^2)$

$94–110^2$.—The alto is charged with this entry in full, making twelve bars. Now that the trill is extended to four crotchets, it heightens the dramatic nature of the Subject. In fact the latent dramatic content of the Subject is seen in this augmentation. Beethoven emphasizes this by accompanying the rest of the Subject a sixth below in the bass.* Meanwhile, the Countersubjects are also augmented. The first Countersubject should have opened on G flat (cf. 27^1), but Beethoven uses the third below the Subject (C flat), instead of the third above. A comparison with 36^1 shows this more plainly. The second Countersubject, however, is at the normal pitch, but is a crotchet late if the augmentation of 36^2 is to be followed strictly. This delay serves the double object of allowing *b* to be heard alone as it begins, which makes the listener more aware of the augmentation, and of enabling the right hand to reach the D natural more comfortably, now that the Countersubjects are over three octaves apart. This wide range makes the music seem to be in four voices for a few bars. After 102^1, Beethoven feels it would be useless to try to make the right hand continue to produce both Countersubjects! However, in 102^2–105, it disjointedly produces *f* in augmentation, punctuating the dramatic *sforzandi* below it. This motif also occurs at its appointed time and pitch in relation to the Subject (cf. 30 f.). The C flats in 96, on which the A flats (98) and F's (100) depend, are then the only exception to the established procedure; their function is primarily to effect a dramatic and protracted interrupted cadence in the new key (94–97^1).

In the ensuing codetta the bass thunders out *f* from 106 to 109 while the upper parts freely imitate *c* and *d* in a rough inversion of 101–105. In $109^3/110^2$ augmentation is kept up, though only of fragments of *f* (soprano) and *b* (alto, copied in sixths in the bass), and this leads to the Answer.

110^3–116^2.—The first impression is that Beethoven is going to produce the Answer in full, but he confines the entry to the more rhythmic part of *a* and *b* and avoids the tedious repetition of the long sequence of quavers. This throws *a* into relief, and

---

* In the bass of 97^1 the second quaver is given in the Original Edition as E [flat]. This is surely a misprint for F, which Busoni, Tovey, and the *Gesamtausgabe* give. There seems no virtue at all in E flat here. Tovey asserts further that there should also be a G flat for the first quaver instead of a rest, which the *Gesamtausgabe* has. Busoni supplies a small note in brackets to remedy the omission.

still more strongly by the augmented inversion in *stretto* in the
bass (111^3 ff.). The full dramatic and structural significance
of the trill is now seen. The alto is a free part, available to complete the harmony ($111^3/112$, where it is derived from *b* and
suggests *h*), and to reinforce the other parts by parallel motion
($114-116$). The limitations of Beethoven's pianoforte, of course,
caused him to omit the low B flat in 114 f.

Episode

116^3-129.—There now follows a series of overlapping versions of *a*, *recto* and *inverso*, with and without the last note of the
motif. The alto of $119^3/120$ suggests *a*, both inverted and
cancrizans :

Ex. 48
Bars 119   120   121

Motif *f* again predominates (125^3-129), as in $80-84$, the bass of
128 f. producing the rhythm of *a* without the leap, which leads
to the next section.

Return of the Material of the Independent Episode

$130-152$.—The motifs begin this time in different voices.
The little bass run (from $85^3/86^1$, bass) now acquires more
significance, both separately and also as a substitute for the
opening of motif *a'* (132^3, alto, and 134^3, bass).   Motif *f'* undergoes variation ($130^2/131^1$, soprano; $133/134^1$, soprano and bass;
135, soprano). Beethoven is careful not to write an exact
repetition of the earlier section. He now builds up a sequence
based on *a'* (soprano) and *f'* (bass) extended to a full octave
scale, with the alto providing the previously accompanimental
motif, now appearing as self-sufficient. At 140 the structure is
inverted, the alto motif eliminated, and the two upper parts
alternate the extensions of *f'*. From 143 the tension is eased;
the alto has quavers beginning with a hint of *a*, which the
soprano loosely imitates, and the bass arpeggios decorate the
octaves that characterize the part from 140, and, in a sense,

from 136. References to the octave scales persist and help the music to fuse imperceptibly into a new treatment of the Subject.

Third Middle Section, Cancrizans (153–174²)

153–161.—The Subject is now treated in *cancrizans* fashion for its full six bars. The tonality of the fugue has progressively become flatter: B flat to 52, D flat to 84, G flat to 90, and E flat minor to 110. The tonality sharpens temporarily to B flat minor to 129 and to A flat to 144, but flattens quickly to D flat (145), G flat (147), and C flat minor (149) which is written as B minor. Above the Subject Beethoven places a third Countersubject which, at first, runs in parallel tenths with the outline of the Subject. This seems to treat the opening leap of *a* harmonically. The first three notes of this Countersubject have even the appearance of the *cancrizans* form of *a*, with the leap reduced to a simple third. It is dangerous to press these similarities too far, but it must be admitted that this Countersubject fits the theme admirably. The harmonic tenths are reduced to a sixth and then thirds,⋆ which are retained even when the parts cross in 157² f. Beethoven carefully makes his Countersubject very simple, in order to set the new form of the Subject into relief. The beautiful smooth line of the Countersubject and its *cantabile* indication give it character and compensating importance.

At 158² the soprano announces *a*, *recto* and direct, recalling a little the precedent of 116³ ff. Beethoven ingeniously joins it to the end of the preceding Countersubject and even makes it hint at *b* in a straightforward statement of the Subject, but soon breaks into free movement which merges into an Answer in D at 162. While awaiting the Answer, alto and bass both quote *a* in quick succession.

162–168.—When inverted with the Subject, the Counter-

⋆ In this Countersubject the tie between the two B's at 156³/157¹ is missing in the Original Edition, according to Ratz, but a tie seems logical from the precedent set in the previous bar. Tovey inserts a tie; Busoni and the *Gesamtausgabe* however, omit it without any comment, and even make one phrase end at 156³ and another begin at 157¹! Ratz and Tovey insert ties and Busoni and the *Gesamtausgabe* omit them at the corresponding points at 163³/166¹ (bass) and 172³/173¹ (alto).

subject produces some $^6_4$ chords (164 f.). In both cases the bass acts as a pedal, which mitigates the $^6_4$ chords. However, reckoning soprano and alto as self-sufficient, no ordinary composer would have been happy with this part-writing over the barline between 165 and 166. The F sharp and G in the soprano of 166[1] are like a decorated resolution of the $^6_4$ chord to the $^5_3$ on the second quaver.

169–174[3].—Just at the end of the Answer the B minor tonality is retrieved, so that the bass can state the Subject again. Beethoven misses no opportunity of fitting in *a*. The alto does this in 167[3]–169[2], while waiting to present the Countersubject. Over the first half of this entry, the soprano presents a beautiful metamorphosis of the current Countersubject. In such a way, Beethoven knits his material into a unified whole.

Episode (174[3]–207)

174[3]–195.—Fragments of the Subject are now juxtaposed. Even *a cancrizans* is disguised in the soprano at 174[3] and the alto at 176[3], but the bass has an unvaried version at 175[3]. At this point the alto slips in a fragment of the third Countersubject. Motif *b cancrizans* joins on to *a* in inversion in the soprano (177 f.), which part continues to fall in thirds, the motto-interval of the sonata. The Episode then concentrates on *b*, which chiefly appears in parallel tenths in two parts. It is inverted in 182 f. At 184 the motif is inverted (soprano), inverted and *cancrizans* (alto) and *recto* and *cancrizans* (bass). Once Beethoven has demonstrated this marvel, the parts relax and become freer again. He never strains at a technical point, as a lesser composer might. In 191, *b* is stripped of its crotchet, so that the semiquavers run continuously. The parts are completely free from 193, though the turns of *c* and *d* are hinted at.

196–207.—The listener is now better able to appreciate a normal entry of the Subject. This is not a Middle Section. Its function seems to be to remind the listener of the original shape of the Subject before it undergoes further transformation. Hence the sixth and least important bar is omitted, and the upper parts are not given the Countersubjects. They have an apparently new rhythm, but it is really only one part made into two. It derives from the alto of 196, as this reconstruction shows:

Ex. 49

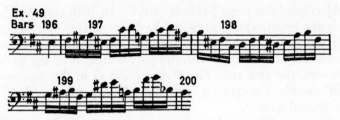

More sequential writing continues the Episode to the next Middle Section.

Soprano and alto separate at 200; the soprano adopts a rhythm of f of the first Countersubject at this point (cf. 30), while the alto introduces a descending arpeggio. These two parts alternate their motifs bar by bar, as the bass treats the fifth bar of the Subject in sequence. As has happened before, Beethoven allows these motifs to be broken into fragments and the tension relaxed before the new entry.

Fourth Middle Section in Inversion (208–222)

208–216[1].—Still another treatment of the Subject is now presented (208 ff., soprano), this time inversion. This treatment is inevitable because of the abundant preparation of *a* from 101 onwards and *b* from 184 onwards. The Subject is stated in full. As the Countersubjects had not appeared in the *cancrizans* Middle Section (153 ff.), when it was sufficient complication that the Subject alone appeared in this way, it is doubly refreshing to find they both return here, also inverted, in the lower parts. However it is only a hint of them; the Subject is clearly the most important thing to Beethoven. They soon break up and go free; evidently, Beethoven wants the listener to attend to the new version of the Subject, while not allowing him to forget the original Countersubjects. Their presence helps the listener to recognize the Subject, though disguised. After a codetta of two bars the Answer appears in the alto, delayed by a beat at 216[2].

216[2]–222.—This statement has the last four crotchets missing, but the soprano of 222 has the essence of them:

Ex. 50

By such means, Beethoven harnesses apparently meandering semiquavers and makes them relevant to his musical argument. During this statement the soprano varies e of the first Countersubject. Again this Countersubject falls instead of rises, so that the third repetition in 219 becomes so altered as to be unrecognizable. The bass does not vary g of the second Countersubject. Too much variation at once would burden the listener. Pianistic considerations cause the rise at $218^3/219^1$. A codetta (221 f.) leads to a lengthy Episode.

Episode (223–249)

223–228.—The principal feature is the inversion of a, at first without the leap, and with the final crotchet decorated (224–228). Beethoven establishes in 223 that he will discuss this motif by writing it normally in the soprano, while the bass indicates what the decoration will be. The minim outline of the soprano in 223–225 is also that of the inversion of a (cf. $208/209^1$, soprano). Against it, the lower parts have motifs that make full closes in each bar. Both are related to earlier motifs, the alto to b and the bass to g. This sequence is then inverted, following Beethoven's frequent practice in this fugue. It is not dryly inverted but made the opportunity for a variation in the soprano.

229–249.—The bass now states a rather belated third entry of the inverted Subject, in a key foreign to that of the earlier entries. This breaks off in the fifth bar. The upper parts move mostly in contrary motion, in the style of b and c. Consecutive fifths occur between soprano and bass in 234^1 but they are not noticeable because of the high speed and the logical movement of the parts.

The Episode proper resumes at 235. The scale passage, arising from 234 (bass), now becomes an apparently new motif, but it is really a filling-in of the leap of a tenth in a. As this is sounded together with the inversion of a, it is the first hint of the simultaneous presentation of the Subject *recto* and *inverso*, which is to come later. In 240, the bass E flat serves the double function of completing a begun in 239 and beginning another statement of it. This happens again in 242. However, from 235 to 242, only the first two notes of a are being discussed. This is shown in their diminution (243–246) though, as Busoni

85

shows,* the alto can virtually be said to include the third note by reason of the harmony in the next chord :

Ex. 51

Bars   243   244   244   245   246

After this excited rise, three-part writing is temporarily abandoned and all three parts move in octaves, leading to a half close in D.

Exposition and Development of Fourth Countersubject

250–278.—Beethoven completely alters the character of the fugue and gives his listener a brief respite from the restless energy, which has been maintained up to this moment without a break. The Subject is laid aside for a few moments while a theme is introduced and given a fugal exposition. The question arises immediately whether this is a second Subject and the fugue is to become a double fugue.

After its exposition, the characteristics of a second Subject in a double fugue are (1) it ends simultaneously with the first Subject when the two are combined and (2) it is a reasonably permanent feature of the rest of the fugue, so justifying its equal importance with the first Subject. These characteristics do not apply to the present theme. A brief examination of the music from 279 shows that the theme ends while the Subject is still dealing with *b*, because it is so short, and it disappears altogether after 292. The fugue is therefore not a double fugue and the theme is not a second Subject. It is really a fourth Countersubject.

Tovey says that such definite counterpoints as this, 'thus established in the mid-course of a fugue, whether in present or destined combination with the Subject, deserve the title of Second or Third Subject, to distinguish them from the ordinary countersubjects of the Exposition'.† This surely misleads by suggesting for a theme an exaggerated importance not intended by the composer and misunderstands its function in the fugue as a whole. It is just as easy and less confusing to number these

* Op. cit., I, 201.   † Op. cit., p. 251.

themes as Countersubjects than as Subjects. Tovey is similarly unfortunate in his terminology when he refers* to the third Countersubject at 153 ff. as a Subject. This has not even been given an independent exposition.

The function of these twenty-nine bars is the military one of *reculer pour mieux sauter*. It is necessary to give the Subject new freshness. This can best be done by abandoning it and its constant rushing for a while, but not for so long that it is forgotten, and by changing the atmosphere of the music. The listener can consolidate his aural impressions of the fugue so far and prepare for the Subject to return with renewed vigour. He does so in the serene calm of smoothly moving crotchets. By retaining a fugal style for this section, Beethoven keeps the listener thinking fugally and links the music that has preceded it with what is to follow. This different treatment of the Countersubject compared with the others probably caused Busoni to describe this section as *Novation*.† It both engages the listener's attention and rests it. The fugal procedure throws into relief the interval of a third, so dear to Beethoven in this sonata, which constitutes the structure of this simple theme:

Ex. 52

Thirds can even be heard in descending outline (*) which recalls the descent of *c* through falls of a third. Nagel's assertion‡ that the principal idea for this Countersubject is derived from the fifth bar of the Subject:

Ex. 53

is quite possible, because a third in the outline of the Subject is being filled in. This filling-in of the third can be constantly seen in this section. After successive entries in the alto and bass,

* Ibid., pp. 250 ff.   † Op. cit., I, 202.

‡ *Beethoven und seine Klaviersonaten*, 2nd edn. (1924), II, 305 f.

87

the point next appears in full in *stretto* (259–263) passing through the same order of parts as at the beginning.*

A motif of this sort is very suitable for sequential treatment, another characteristic of the present fugue. The bass shows this first at 264, when the third bar is repeated in sequence. This outlines the descent in thirds still more (*):

Ex. 54

There is a striking resemblance between the soprano of 262–265 and the essential melodic movement of 24–27:

Ex. 55

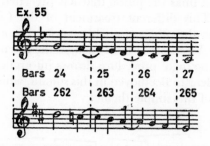

| Bars | 24 | 25 | 26 | 27 |
| Bars | 262 | 263 | 264 | 265 |

At 265^2 the bass again imitates a sequence, now rising, which the soprano continues (267^2–270^1). The soprano of 270–271^1 gives the outline only of the opening of the Countersubject.

---

* According to Ratz, the naturals are missing before the C's in the soprano and bass of 262. He says that the *stretto* entries in descending fifths are the chief evidence for the correctness of C natural. He means, presumably, that because the second and fourth notes are the same in both soprano and alto entries, the bass should do likewise. This is possible, but not conclusive. The alto and bass entries here are at the same pitch as the soprano and alto entries at 250 ff. At that point, Beethoven distinctly gives a C sharp to the alto (253^2). A stronger argument for the C naturals in 262 is that by the beginning of this bar Beethoven has modulated to G major, and they help to consolidate and maintain this key to the end of 264. C sharps would destroy G major with an immediate modulation. Though the case for C naturals seems stronger, a final decision will probably never be possible. This doubt can be seen in other editions. Busoni has (♮)♯ before each C and Tovey gives [♮] before the note and a small ♯? above it in each case. The *Gesamtausgabe*, however, disregards the dispute with a definite sharp before both C's.

The *stretto* effect is again secured from 269², but not so exactly this time. As if in compensation, Beethoven ingeniously writes the bass of 271²–273 to give the effect of four-part writing. The soprano (272) seems to take over the bass entry of 271², while the final bass entry is more complete. From 275 Beethoven modulates wonderfully and naturally to use this latest Countersubject in conjunction with the Subject.

Fourth Countersubject and Opening of Subject combined in Double Fugato style

279–294¹.—The Countersubject has been so striking in its simplicity that it still holds the attention despite the presence of the Subject. The latter seems fussy and timid, not daring to compete with the Countersubject. In fact the Countersubject seems to become a main theme to which the Subject acts as countersubject. However, when it gains prominence and can be recognized as the original Subject, it sounds delightfully fresh. Only *a* and *b* are quoted by the alto, by which time the abbreviated fourth Countersubject has finished. The bass then gives four bars of the Subject at 282 ff., and two partial statements of the Countersubject by the alto and soprano fit with it.

By 286 the dynamics have increased so that the soprano entry sounds more forceful. As if to prevent the Subject regaining its predominance too soon, Beethoven breaks it up and uses only a part of *b*. A sequence follows, in which this remnant of *b* is set in 2-crotchet rhythm against the 3-crotchet rhythm of the second bar of the fourth Countersubject in octaves. The Countersubject becomes a mere accompanimental device and, as such, is allowed to disappear at 292³, having served its purpose; this is a further reason for not regarding it as a Subject in its own right.

The shortened form of the Subject in this section serves a number of purposes, (1) it helps to reintroduce the theme gradually, (2) it is long enough to establish the relationship with the fourth Countersubject both in their derivation from the interval of a third and also in combination, and (3) it suggests treatment in *stretto* which is now to be exploited.

Fifth Middle Section in Stretto with Subject in Direct Form and Inversion

294²–305.—The *stretto* of the Subject, *recto* and *inverso*, first seen (in augmentation) in 110³ ff., is now produced almost in full in normal note-lengths. Neither entry begins on the first beat of the bar, but precedents for this have already been established (47³ and 65²). The inverted Subject leads, followed a beat later by the direct Answer, and as Tovey points out,* this is the converse of the *stretto* in augmentation in which the direct Subject led. This entry does not work too well, for the harmony in 296 f. is not particularly happy.† Suddenly, in 298³, Beethoven makes the bass fit the alto in a mirror version of the end of *c* and all *d*. Mirror treatment brings the climax to Beethoven's use of technical devices in this fugue.

This mixture of close *stretto* and mirror treatment is repeated in the answering entry at 300². As before, the inverted theme leads, again in Subject form, followed this time by the direct Subject. In the soprano of 302 f., Beethoven finds a drop of a third works better than a fourth. The liberty is transferred to the bass (303), where the gap is narrowed to a second, and, in the present tonal context of E flat, this gives a refreshing effect of an interrupted cadence. The change to mirror treatment occurs at the corresponding place in 304³. Beethoven allows himself distinct liberties with the Subject in this section. Perhaps these are some of the *licenze* to which he refers in his heading.

Episode

306–333.—The mirror treatment of *c* and *d* continues to 307². From 307³, *a* in inversion is marked out for special emphasis in the alto. The first note has to be elided the second and third time, as follows:

Ex. 56

* Op. cit., p. 254.

† In 297², Busoni for no obvious reason replaces the crotchet C in the bass with a crotchet rest. This may be a printer's error. All other editions give the crotchet C.

In fact, the soprano provides this missing note, and so at 310^3 it is ready to take over the sequence, while the bass adopts the soprano's semiquavers. The free part (308 ff., bass, and 311 ff., alto) is a variation of the inversion of *a* in Answer form. The parts are rearranged again in 313^3 ff. and the sequence continues. Exigencies of keyboard-writing in these last bars prevent the soprano having the same free part.

The dominant pedal (318 ff.) hints at the end of the fugue, and the upper texture looks back on earlier material. Motif *f* returns in the soprano, over semiquavers derived from *d*. There are two soprano parts in 303 and 305, the lower of which accompanies the alto in sixths. This is a licence certainly, but the ear accepts the music still as in three parts because of the pedal. The two-bar pattern of 303 f. is repeated sequentially in 305 f. and then, following Beethoven's custom, it is inverted. A full inversion would have given the soprano a held F in 307, but this, apart from making the alto more difficult to play, would have over-emphasized the pedal idea too soon. It is omitted, and the occasion used for an imitation with the bass in 308. The imitation in the sequence is not stressed in full any more because Beethoven now works towards a climax. Instead, the soprano takes over the semiquavers which begin with an exact replica of almost all the last two bars of the Subject and continue with a succession of inverted turns. Motif *f* is compressed into one bar in 325^3 ff. and later becomes fragmented first in the alto (328^3 ff.) and then in the soprano and bass (330^3 ff.).

The final chord of 332 is a diminished seventh, which is used in 333 for a simultaneous statement of *a, recto* and *inverso*. Soprano and alto have the motif in Answer form with the tritone leap; the bass, in thirds like the alto, has the Subject form with the leap of a tenth.

Final Section (334–366)

334–344.—The diminished seventh chord is not immediately resolved, but is continued during 334 while the alto repeats the soprano an octave lower, resolves normally, and continues a statement of the Answer in the original key for five bars* to

---

* In the alto of 335^2 Schenker gives the last semiquaver as E natural without comment. Indeed, no comment seems necessary because the note

338. The soprano takes over the sixth bar an octave higher in 339. With this entry the soprano recapitulates the first Countersubject as long as the alto has the Answer, but the bass has only two bars of the second Countersubject (335 f.) and then is silent until its ponderous entry at 345.

A sequence of 338 f. follows as a codetta from 340, in which the alto and soprano continue to share the last two bars of the Subject against the first bar of f, which was neglected in 325 ff. The inverted turn returns in 343^3 f. as it had done in 327 ff. Busoni's theory* that the idea behind 343^3–344^1 was:

Ex. 57

has little probability. One could do the same thing with 344^{2-3} for the same reason, and the total effect would not be what Beethoven wrote at all. He always wrote what he thought, and Busoni seems to have assumed too much here.

345–358.—Beethoven has previously given a mirror version of the Subject from near the end of c in 298^3 ff. and again in 304^3 f. The Episode continues in the same vein in 306 f. Now, all the remainder of the Subject is similarly treated and the mirroring of the Subject is discontinued at exactly the same point as the previous mirroring began. In other words, all the Subject has now been heard in simultaneous inversion with itself. The trill in the soprano's a is converted into normal notation in 345^{2-3} and the alto begins the inverted first Countersubject in 346. It is quite possible and indeed probable that, as he was composing 345 ff., Beethoven found that a continuation of the mirror version after 348^3 would repeat the substance of 298^3 ff. A great advantage that accrues from breaking off the Subject in the middle is that the opening of the Subject can appear instead. This gives the effect of *stretto*

is E natural in the original Answer. No other form of E is used either in the Answer or in this entry or in the accompanying first Countersubject. Both Busoni and Tovey, however, have unaccountable doubts. Though they give E natural, they both add a flat above the note for no real or stated reason. The *Gesamtausgabe*, on the other hand, gives an unequivocal flat before the E.

* Op. cit., I, 204.

which is maintained to greater or less degree as the prevailing atmosphere of the rest of the fugue.

The bass of 349^1 is rewritten to allow the left hand to bring in the abbreviated Subject in the alto. The interchanged accidentals in the soprano of 351^{2-3} reduce the leap of the Answer in effect to a tenth, like the Subject form of a. The tonality is temporarily switched to C minor, checked strongly by the bass at 353^2 as it makes an entry. More liberties are now being taken with the Subject. Motif b does not leap a fourth in the normal place, but continues its scale to make a run of a tenth and then leaps (353^3–356^3). This is slightly reminiscent of 235–238. These scales, in which *stretto* of b at a crotchet's distance is implied as Busoni clearly shows,* are prominent until the next entry in the soprano at 359.

359–366.—This entry is the highest in the fugue and gives a sense of supreme achievement. This is the climax of the fugue. The entry, though in the tonic, is set in Answer form. It is the final entry and is almost complete. Bass and alto have a in 360 ff. and then the second Countersubject emerges at 362^2, followed by all but the first note of f of the first Countersubject in the bass. This note, the quaver F, is supplied by the alto, after which this part accompanies the motif a third higher.

Once more Beethoven inverts the material (364^3–366^2). The bass has bar 5 of the Subject twice with a small modification, while f is broken up in the soprano and alto. A final cadence ends the fugue proper, after which three-part writing is hard to trace.

Coda (367–400)

367–384^2.—Fragments of the Subject are now gathered up into a mighty conclusion. Motif a is heard very tentatively again in *stretto*, *recto* and *inverso* (367^2 ff.) and mirrored in the alto (368^{2-3}). From 369^2, the bass extends the trill by nearly three bars, making an E flat pedal, above which the diminished seventh chord, built on this E flat, is displayed in arpeggios. At 372^3 the trill moves to the dominant with the unusual procedure of a further tonic pedal above.

Over this double pedal the alto has the first four bars of the Subject, while the soprano has e and g rolled into one, as in

* Ibid., I, 204 f.

96^2 ff. The second Countersubject motif is now in its proper rhythmical place in relation to the Subject, but a third lower than it would be normally. Motif e is a fifth lower. In 377 ff., alto and soprano again imitate each other in a variation of f. The pace slackens, helped by repeated low F's in the bass, as the thickened upper parts move from 379^3 to a form of interrupted cadence, with a uppermost. Inversion of the structure again occurs in 382.

384^2–400.—The original *tempo* resumes with b, which gathers momentum and rushes down the scale to 389, where all three parts give out a in octaves. It is now set in a succession of $\frac{4}{4}$ bars, which displaces the rhythm by a crotchet each time. This very cleverly recapitulates the three different positions in the bar in which Beethoven has presented this motif during the fugue. By 397 full chords are used, as a in Answer form, as at 359, reaches the final height and final cadence.

VII

FINALE, PIANOFORTE SONATA IN
A FLAT, OP. 110 (1821)

Principal Editions:

1. *Klaviersonaten*, pp. 588–90, 592–4 (Vol. IV).
2. *Die letzten fünf Sonaten von Beethoven* (*Erläuterungsausgabe*), *Op.*
   110.
3. *Sonatas for Pianoforte*, III, 228–31, 232–5.
4. *Gesamtausgabe*, XVI, iii. 123–4, 126–8 (Nr. 154).

AFTER a serenely lyrical first movement and a turbulent
scherzo for a second movement, the finale of this sonata combines the functions of slow and fast movements in alternation.
With the speed *Adagio*, the movement opens in B flat minor
which seems a natural outcome from the F major (*Tierce de
Picardie*) ending of the second movement and moves to one of
Beethoven's rare examples of instrumental recitative. The structure of the rest of the movement, and particularly the fugue, is
very unusual. Schenker's convincing reasons* for this suggest
Beethoven's probable train of thought in arriving at the final
outline of its composition and it will be helpful to summarize
them here.

Beethoven wanted to overcome the inherent division between
an Adagio and a Finale and raise them to a powerful unity.
He solves this novel problem by making the fugue the truly

* H. Schenker, *Die letzten fünf Sonaten von Beethoven*, *Op. 110*, 1914,
pp. 49 f., 58 f., and 67.

dominating section and embodying in it the desired unity at the same time. He can achieve this only by reducing the two *Arioso* sections to their formal function as the elements of an Adagio. The *Arioso* sections show their subservience by being adapted to the tonal needs of the fugue.

As the *Arioso* is given in two parts, so too is the fugue. The majority of fugues consist essentially of three sections: (1) an exposition, announcing chiefly the tonic key, (2) a middle section, using the contrast of various other keys, and (3) a final section, returning to the tonic key as the counterpart of the exposition. How this scheme can best be divided into *two* parts is a difficult problem. Only Beethoven, with his knowledge of fugue, based rather on deep, personal needs than on text-books, could do this, and still leave it undamaged as a true fugue.

The fundamental question is whether the Middle Section should be added to the Exposition or to the Final Section. Beethoven's solution is to let the Exposition stand alone and join the other two sections together as the second and latter part of the fugue. This cannot be done without making some concessions, but these are justified by their inherent necessity and in the corresponding elasticity in the form, discovered so ingeniously by Beethoven. A second problem now arises: how to give the Exposition the force of an independent section. The usual three entries (or four with a redundant entry) are not enough. It must be expanded. How many entries are needed to give just the right length? In what key should they appear? Finally, how can the section be made to seem both an independent whole, and at the same time the Exposition?

Beethoven solves the problem in this way: (1) he makes three cycles of three entries each, together with intervening sections of various lengths, all of which gives sufficient content; had the theme been more expanded, a nine-fold statement would have had the worst imaginable effect, (2) as the entries in an exposition are in either the tonic or the dominant, so it is here with all these nine entries, with one exception, and (3) he emphasizes the Exposition as a self-sufficient section by putting the first entry of the 3rd cycle in D flat, and by using *stretti* and a pedal-point. These last points are the concessions previously referred to.

After the return of the *Arioso*, the Middle and Final Sections of the fugue are taken up. It would be logical to expect all three voices to be active at the resumption, and not to begin the Middle Section like the beginning of a fugue with an un-accompanied entry. On the other hand, the division of the fugue into two parts requires that the second section should begin as if the fugue were starting just at this point and that it had not been previously interrupted. Beethoven deals with this by making the revival of strength (*poi a poi di nuovo vivente*) from the plaintive *Arioso* the opportunity for bringing in one voice at a time like an exposition. There is no doubt that it is the Middle Section from its use of various keys, inversion, augmentation, and diminution.

This commentary by Schenker seems to be the most reliable guide to the structure of the movement.

The Sketches and Autographs

Both Nottebohm and Schenker have studied the sketch-book that contains much of Beethoven's preliminary work for this sonata. According to Nottebohm,* this sketch-book contains eighty-eight pages,† of which pages 64–88 are devoted to the work. Unfortunately he quotes only one sketch for the fugue:

Ex. 58

This shows the Subject in its final form apart from the last note. How much effort this had already entailed Beethoven one cannot tell; Nottebohm does not say. Possibly Beethoven may have had less difficulty with this Subject, because it is obviously planned on the same outline as the opening theme of the first movement (Ex. 59).

---

* G. Nottebohm, 'Drei Skizzenhefte aus den Jahren 1819 bis 1822', *Zweite Beethoveniana*, pp. 463 ff.

† 'Seiten'; this suggests a sketch-book of 44 leaves.

Ex. 59

The later substitution of the held C for the quavers at the end of the Subject gives the music, if anything, poise for the new entry.

Schenker is even less communicative. Because of the excessive quantity of material he refrains from presenting fully the history of the origin of the fugue.[*] The only sketch he mentions is the end of the one Nottebohm reproduces. According to Schenker it occurs on page 69 of the sketch-book.[†]

Nagel, in his commentary on the sonata, reproduces[‡] the same sketches as Nottebohm, except that the first one is shown as follows:

Ex. 60

This is almost certainly a misprint for C at *, as Nagel represents[§] it as being already in the final form except for the slight deviation at the end, already mentioned.

It is interesting to note that Beethoven was also trying out the inversion of the Subject. Without clefs or key-signatures one must assume this was meant to be also in A flat major. To use this key for the experiment of inversion is a matter of convenience here and does not necessarily mean that he was intending it as the key of the Middle Section. The eventual setting of the inversion in G major stems from the unwritten harmonic change of the dominant seventh chord on E flat at $113^2/114^1$ into a German sixth chord on E flat, which moves to a $^6_4$ chord

---

[*] Op. cit., p. 62.

[†] 'Blatt 69'; Schenker must, on this occasion, be numbering both sides of each leaf, like Nottebohm.

[‡] W. Nagel, *Beethoven und seine Klaviersonaten*, 2nd edn. (1924), II, 361 f., 367.

[§] Ibid., p. 361.

of G minor. G minor governs the whole second appearance of the *Arioso*, and becomes G major for the continuation of the fugue.

Schenker deserves our gratitude, however, for discussing many interesting differences in the texts of two autograph scores and another copy revised and corrected by Beethoven. These scores are* (1) Beethoven's first complete autograph, in the Royal Library, later known as the Öffentliche Wissenschaftliche Bibliothek, and now as the Deutsche Staatsbibliothek, Berlin, (2) Beethoven's second autograph, which contains only the third movement, that is, the Adagio and Fugue, then (August 1914) in the possession of Herr Louis Koch, of Frankfurt, but now in the collection of the late Hans C. Bodmer, Zürich, and (3) a copy, revised by Beethoven, from Brahms's collection, in the Gesellschaft der Musikfreunde, Vienna. They give a good insight into Beethoven's way of thinking in the final stages of composition. His highly self-critical standards are always present in his attempts to reach perfection.

In the first autograph, 62 appeared thus:†

Ex. 61

This was changed in the second autograph to:‡

Ex, 62

The aural impression of Ex. 61 is that the E flat in the right hand begins a fourth voice while the previous highest part has a

* H. Schenker, op. cit., p. 2.   † Ibid., p. 60.   ‡ Ibid., p. 61.

continuous descent of quavers. The introduction of a fourth voice had to be avoided and so now the entry is prepared by a preliminary E flat. Strictly, the parts cross here, but as they remain so, it is best to regard the two upper parts as having interchanged and write their stems accordingly. The third copy has a different version of this bar:*

Ex. 63

In this, the suspension of the middle part has been eliminated. Past editors have been divided over these versions; some have preferred Beethoven's autograph rather than his revised copy, others have obeyed the revision as being his final thought. Schenker chooses Ex. 62 because it prevents the middle part from being rhythmically heavy and monotonous and the E flat from being heard too loudly before the entry on another E flat. This view seems misguided. One part cannot be considered by itself in this way. The sounding of the E flat on the first beat need not spoil the effectiveness of the entry, especially as it is an inner part and an octave lower than the entry. Moreover, Ex. 63 simplifies the harmony which, at that register and speed, was too complicated. On only two other occasions in the fugue do all three parts move on each quaver of a beat, by simple contrary motion in 87 and for the climax in 109. This consideration may have prompted Beethoven's revision, which ought to stand.

For 78 ff. Beethoven writes in the first autograph:†

Ex. 64

* H. Schenker, op. cit., p. 62.   † Ibid., p. 63.

This is musically the content of 78, 80, and 81. The avoidance of a rosalia is Beethoven's only advantage here, but the resultant monotonous bass rhythm of seven bars is a greater disadvantage. In the same autograph he makes the correction of adding 79, to give the final version. The rosalia is the obvious solution and the rhythmic monotony of the bass is removed by the introduction of quavers which intensify the climax to 79.

A very interesting set of revisions follows now. Six bars later in the first autograph, Beethoven writes the entry in A flat instead of the later D flat,* though the two G flats give a strong feeling of the latter key:

Ex. 65

The subdominant (D flat) is needed in order to give a sense of finality to the Exposition as an independent section, and this shows Beethoven's early intention of using the key to accompany the Subject in its original form. The more important weakness at present is that the pedal begins too soon, and so he expands the passage from * to:†

Ex. 66

This revision is made in the course of writing out the movement in the first autograph. Notwithstanding the difficulty
Beethoven had with this section, the music following the pedal
is essentially in its final form in the first autograph.

In this autograph which occupies fifty-two pages, all entries
in the Exposition are in either tonic or dominant which shows
that Beethoven originally wanted to confine the section to these
keys as being most fitting. After the final chord on page 52,
he makes an extensive sketch in pencil to improve this last
section further:*

Ex. 67

The chief difference is the introduction of an incomplete entry
in D flat at the beginning. This more prominent use of the subdominant suggests that Beethoven considered that merely to
harmonize the Subject in D flat was not strong enough to
prepare the end of the Exposition. It is also too similar to other

* H. Schenker, op. cit., p. 63.

places in the Exposition where there have been temporary modulations to D flat, or its relative minor, B flat minor. A greater contrast can only be obtained by putting an actual entry into the subdominant. This is done at first in an experimental manner. The abbreviated entry, almost hidden in the middle of the texture, draws as little attention to itself as possible, and is immediately supplemented by the Subject in the soprano with a hint of *stretto* two bars later in the bass. This version satisfies Beethoven for a time, and the sketch, nearly indecipherable, is used in almost the same form in the second autograph. Later, however, he considered the pedal still insufficiently prepared. A further sketch in the first autograph, page 55, shows the final version with the full statement of the entry in D flat. This not only expands the passage further but also gives the needed feeling of finality to the whole Exposition by shifting more firmly to the subdominant. Its gradual arrival into the fugue shows that it could not be considered as a middle entry. It is interesting to note that this sketch was not also carried forward to the second autograph. The second autograph represents therefore the state of the composition at one of its final stages, but one must continue to refer to the first autograph for further alterations.

Accordingly, the first autograph goes on to show that Beethoven is now dissatisfied with the immediate approach to the pedal, especially in the upper parts. Another sketch follows★ on pages 55 f.:

Ex. 68

This involves the old mistake of introducing the pedal too soon and it is difficult to see why Beethoven wrote it like this. He has crossed out the premature pedal as if aware of the mistake and rewritten the passage on the last page of the first autograph★ (Ex. 69).

★ Ibid., p. 64.

Ex. 69

The upper parts of the last two bars are, harmonically, a succession of thirds. Beethoven removes this monotony in the final version with an alternation of thirds and sixths (cf. the previous three bars) but with the position of the thirds and sixths reversed in relation to the barline.

On page 39 of the first autograph, 106 ff. appear as:*

Ex. 70

The top note (A flat) is held rather too long while the bass plods through its entry in *stretto* with the upper part. Beethoven feels more urgency is required as an extremely sketchy pencil-draft in the margin at this point suggests. This is used in the second autograph, thus:*

* H. Schenker, op. cit., p. 64.

Ex. 71

The final version, including the dynamics, is worked out later on page 56 of the first autograph.

There are two previous versions in the first autograph of the transition to the *Arioso*. The first is on page 39 and in the second autograph:*

Ex. 72

The second appears on page 41 and shows Beethoven thinking of it as an enharmonic modulation:*

Ex. 73

* Ibid., p. 66.

Earlier versions of 163/164 appear in the first autograph:*

Ex. 74(a)

Ex. 74(b)

In the first autograph, 168 ff. appeared on pages 53 and 54 as follows:†

Ex, 75

Pencil sketches interspersed here show corrections pointing to the final form and also indicating Beethoven's very firm intention of moving to the Final Section with a succession of com-

* H. Schenker, op. cit., p. 68.   † Ibid., p. 69.

plete diminutions of the Subject. This would be impracticable because a complete diminution occupies slightly more than half a bar. Beethoven wisely abandons this idea and leaves an abbreviated diminution which is equally powerful in its suggestion.

The version of the upper parts of 174^2 ff. in the first autograph, pages 54 ff.:*

Ex. 76(a)

can be simplified to:

Ex. 76 (b)

The final version, by its insistence on the notes of the Subject of the fugue on each quaver, makes the fact that the middle part really has the Subject more evident.

For the bass of 187^2, Beethoven wrote in the first autograph:†

Ex. 77(a)

He corrects this with notes and letters to:

Ex. 77 (b)

which is confirmed in the second autograph.† In this way he eliminates the A flat suspended from the first beat and makes clearer his real two-part intentions:

Ex. 77(c)

The chromatic rise in the bass of this bar is also heard better.

The harmony of the three beats from 188² to 189² is constant and, as Schenker points out,★ it was very natural for Beethoven to have D flat as the first note of the bass of 189¹. Consequently, Schenker believes D flat is correct here. Several editors, however, give F, probably because Beethoven wrote *simili* instead of notes in the second autograph,† and they assumed that the notes of 188² were to be repeated twice in 189. While Schenker's suggestion of D flat appeals to musical reason, it would have been interesting if he had said what happens in the copy revised by Beethoven.

In both first and second autographs, the bass of 190² is given as:†

Ex. 78

Beethoven changes the second B to A flat in the second autograph, confirming it with a letter *a* (i.e., A flat, allowing for the key-signature) and a cryptic marginal remark, 'ob in Berlin a' ('if in Berlin A [flat]').† A flat is preferable, though B need not be regarded as an error. The Original Edition has B instead of A flat, and this has been copied by other later editions.

In the bass of 191¹, the first autograph has:†

Ex. 79

Beethoven decides that the A natural is too distracting and later substitutes B flat.†

In the first autograph at 192¹ Beethoven writes in the bass:†

Ex. 80

This Alberti pattern is the same as that for the beat before and after it. Beethoven avoids this monotony with an A natural instead of the second E flat; this correction is made in the first autograph and confirmed in the second.*

Finally, at 193^2, the first autograph has for the bass:*

Ex. 81

There is a + by the D flat and the letter *e* (i.e., E flat). In the margin is a written ∓, again with the mysterious 'ob in Berlin?' The E (flat) is incorporated into the second autograph without comment.* Schenker sees that Beethoven wanted to have a dominant seventh chord with the upper parts here, but fails to see what advantage results musically. Beethoven makes a harmonic point at the expense of the counterpoint. Schenker earns sympathy for his disagreement with Beethoven but praise for retaining his corrections. Every semiquaver is important in the Final Section, because it may determine the harmonic implications of the passage or the contrapuntal movement of the parts.

The Fugue

Exposition $(26^2–114^1)$. *First Cycle of Entries* $(26^2–45^1)$

$26^2–30^1$.—Besides the connexion of the Subject thematically to the opening theme of the first movement (see Ex. 59), it resembles also the striding outline which opens Variation V of the finale of the Sonata in E, Op. 109:

Ex. 82

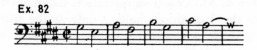

The setting of *Et expecto* in the Mass in D is also very similar in shape (Ex. 83).

* Ibid., p. 74.

Ex. 83

It is noteworthy that all these compositions were occupying Beethoven about the same time and that all three are marked *Allegro ma non troppo*. It seems clear that this theme had a great significance for him. Incidentally, it may be mentioned that the opening theme of the Sonata in E, Op. 14, No. 1, is similar and is also marked *Allegro*.

The Subject consists essentially of two motifs, *a*, an open, rising fourth, heard three times in sequence, and *b*, a complementary filled-in, falling fourth, which combine to give a very satisfactory outline:

Ex. 84

The rhythm in *b* introduces an element of freshness and gives just sufficient relief from the steady dotted crotchets.

30^2–36^1.—While the middle part gives out a real Answer the bass makes a counterpoint in third species with it. This Countersubject follows the outline of the Answer in tenths and so intensifies it. Movement in quavers is maintained virtually throughout the Exposition, halting only at the trill at 110^1, and they provide a constant background against which the fugue-theme stands in relief.

The codetta (34^2–36^1) introduces the idea of syncopation and suspension which is used so extensively in this fugue, and is so necessary in a framework largely of dotted crotchets against quavers which could easily become tedious. Though it modulates to D flat in 35^2/36^1, Beethoven neatly avoids making it permanent by the chromatic D natural and B natural in 36^2.

36^2–45^1.—The Countersubject is not rigidly adhered to melodically or rhythmically, yet the predominant quavers of the middle part in 36^2 ff. make the new form akin to the original. It quickly absorbs the new elements of syncopation and suspension and shortens its leaps of a fourth to the first two quavers of 37 and 38. Fourths can also be traced in the free part, though the last one results from the cadence of 39^2/40^1:

Ex. 85

The last three notes of *b* are here given more prominence. The material of the original codetta is now repeated and extended in sequence, touching on the relative minor at 44^1, with a quick succession of dominant seventh chords in 45 leading to A flat major.

Second Cycle of Entries $(45^2$–$87^2)$

45^2–53^1.—The entries in this cycle are in the reverse order: Answer, Subject, Answer, and balance the first cycle like a counter-exposition. The order of the voices remains the same. The bass states the Answer in octaves in pianistic style from 45^2. The soprano maintains a closer likeness to the original Counter-subject. However, instead of being a true inversion and therefore running in parallel sixths with the Answer, it is still moving in thirds with it. At 48 it takes up the syncopated style heard first in the bass at 35^2. In this way, the two styles of quaver movement are now more noticeably combined in the course of one voice. Now that the two outside parts have come so closely together, the middle part is temporarily squeezed out and put on top while it fills in the harmonies.

The familiar sequence based on *b* recurs in 49^2 ff. The last three notes of *b* are transformed in the bass into the context of syncopation from 51^2 and continued in a downward sequence in tenths with the soprano to the beginning of the next entry.

53^2–62^1.—With the return of the Subject, the original Countersubject reappears in the bass, accompanied for two bars in the soprano. When this has been stated, Beethoven carefully avoids monotony of treatment in the new codetta, by making the middle part concentrate on the last three notes of *b* for its sequence material. It serves to show the importance of this one rhythm in the Subject, especially as the bass takes up the idea in 59–61, while it rests from its quavers. The tied dotted crotchets are given simultaneously to the soprano, so that there remains an aural connexion with those in the previous codettas. In 59–61, the soprano has an apparent sequence, but each bar is slightly different from the others. This is an ingenious variation that might have eluded a lesser composer.

62^2–66^1.—The whereabouts of the parts becomes confused aurally as a new entry begins while the soprano goes lower and lower, becoming the middle part. The ear accepts the music as still three-part writing, since the entry is prepared by the middle part with the last quaver of 62^1. Neither of the lower parts produces the Countersubject at the original pitch for this entry. For pianistic reasons the middle part could not go any lower to accompany it in tenths as in 31–33^1, and the distance of a third would reduce the effectiveness of the entry. The bass could have had the original Countersubject an octave lower, but Beethoven prefers to secure variety by setting it at a different pitch to give the fugue theme a new harmonization.

66^2–87^1.—It has already been pointed out in the discussion on the construction of the fugue that the intervening sections between the entries help to build up the Exposition into an independent whole. Already the four codettas have accounted for two-fifths of these first forty bars. Now follows a section of twenty-one bars which resembles an episode in its proportions. At 66^2, the old form of sequential codetta reappears, varied now into an upward sequence. Some tension is apparent, which is natural after six entries always in either tonic or dominant. The bass helps with a chromatic rise: E flat, E, F, F sharp, G (66^2–70^1). The sequential motif, *b*, in the soprano, is three-fold, with a dramatic leap of a diminished seventh between the second and third statements. Here the quaver rest is vital to heighten the emphasis, particularly as the third statement is freely extended to 74^1. Schenker rightly calls it 'very eloquent';* it is certainly a touch of Beethoven's genius.

The first impression gained from 73 ff. is that, at last, here is

* 'Überaus beredt' (op. cit., p. 61).

a Middle Section. Now is the right moment; but this is not a conventional fugue, nor is Beethoven a conventional composer. If 73 ff. are heard as shown below, then the bass will not be considered as introducing a Middle Section:

This passage emphasizes in no uncertain manner the soaring and exultant nature of the Subject. In case the continuous dotted crotchets should tire the ear, Beethoven ingeniously adds a rhythm in the bass of 79, which foreshadows the crotchet-plus-quaver rhythm of 81^2 ff.

At 80, the bass rises a second on each beat, instead of each bar, as previously. This steeper rise is the basis of the extension of the sequence (80 ff.), which now gives the crotchet-plus-quaver rhythm full scope. The outline of these bars is:

The tied notes are extended too, and form two-bar pedals.

Throughout this section the two motifs of the Subject are constantly used, together with Countersubject figurations using both forms of quaver movement. In fact every element of the music so far is drawn on.

Third Cycle of Entries (87^2-114^1)

87^2-101^1.—The exceptional entry in the subdominant begins this cycle, and though it is given to the middle part it lies above the soprano and so receives considerable prominence. This is tempered by the free counterpoint of the soprano and bass which is based only in style on the Countersubject and by the fact that the soprano restores the tonality immediately with the Subject at 91^2. A strong hint of *stretto* in the bass, two bars later, confirms the tonic key.

Still another type of sequence follows in 95^2 ff. The soprano is built on *b*, moulded into the crotchet-plus-quaver rhythm, while the middle part has familiar quaver movement. This leads straight into the pedal, over which the counterpoint of the two upper parts is inverted to continue the sequence. The solid E flat pedal for nearly three bars serves still further to reassert the tonality, temporarily disturbed by the D flat entry.

101^2-114^1.—The final entry in octaves in the bass is very reminiscent of the bass entry at the beginning of the second cycle $(45^2$ ff.). Above it are free, but derivative, counterpoints. The middle part hints at *stretto* two bars later following the example of the bass in 93^2 ff. At 105^2 the soprano begins the Subject and adds to the effect of *stretto*, but *a* becomes shortened in these closing bars of the Exposition. The bass joins in from 107^1 in this diminution of *a*, as the music reaches its inevitable climax at 110^2 with a dominant seventh chord on E flat. This is extended to 114^1. The Exposition is over and the fugue is laid aside while the *Arioso* is resumed.

The *Arioso* continues for some 22 bars (114^2-136^1), towards the end of which the music moves from G minor to G major in which key the Middle Section of the fugue is taken up. As was shown in the preliminary discussion, Beethoven tried to portray the gradual return of vigour after the grief of the *Arioso* by introducing one voice at a time.

Middle Section in Inversion, Diminution, and Augmentation
   (136^2–174^1)

136^2–151.—Especially with Beethoven's mark *L'inversione della Fuga* it is not difficult to be aware of the inversion of the Subject at the outset in the middle part, followed by an appropriate Answer in the soprano at 140^2. Whatever shape had been adopted for the Answer, three successive drops of a fourth could not have been maintained. By increasing the final drop of *a* to a fifth, Beethoven draws the least attention possible to the change. That both a fourth and a fifth are Perfect intervals contributes to the aural satisfaction. There is no attempt to make the Countersubject follow an inversion. Again there is a mixture of the tied and untied quavers, recalling only the style of the Countersubject. Immediately follows the third statement of the inversion in the bass from 144^2. A fourth entry, in the soprano, follows on the third just as promptly as did the other entries in their turn. The end of *b* in the third entry had been omitted, which gives the impression of a codetta in $147^2/148^1$. The middle part of 147 hints at that type of syncopation which has been heard occasionally before, e.g., in 48^1, 65^1, 105^1, and 144^2. The new entry displays a further metamorphosis, compared with that beginning at 140^2. The notes are altered to make it fit C minor, a passing note is added in 150^1 which suggests the rhythm of *b*, and the ending in $151/152^1$ is still less recognizable. In fact, what can be traced of *b* here is no longer inverted. The bass, with the usual quaver movement for the Countersubject, has a slightly different shape for its sequential motif and ignores the ties.

152–168^1.—A diminution of the Subject, *recto*, begins in the bass immediately at the end of the last inverted entry, each note a third of the original length, with a suitable modification of the rhythm of *b* into semiquavers. The other parts are silent, as if to allow this diminution to be more plainly heard. The last three notes (153^1) seem to echo the same notes at the end of the soprano entry (151^1 f.).

The middle part carries on the diminution, contracting *a* to a third (153^1 f.). Then comes another entry with thirds and fourths combined in the bass of 154^1 f., echoed by a similar one in the middle part in 155^1 f. Normal fourths return in the bass entry at 156^1, with its deceptive anacrusis in the previous beat. In these diminutions the character of the Subject is quite altered because accents now occur on the first, fourth, and seventh notes of an entry, instead of the second, fourth, sixth, and ninth notes. Therefore only the second accent in each case occurs at the same point in both the Subject and its diminution.

During the diminutions, the soprano has been giving an augmentation of the Subject in even note-lengths, so that the diminutions act as decorative counterpoints to it. The lower parts become gradually more fragmentary, using the end of the diminution. This increases the frequency of semiquavers, and continues the feeling of *poi e poi di nuovo vivente*. In fact, the whole section is growing organically out of the original material and is supremely well organized.

There is another diminution (158^2 f., bass) before the roles are reversed at 160^2. The bass announces the next entry which acts as an Answer to the other augmentation. Above this, diminutions are heard simultaneously in the upper parts. The tied note, tentatively introduced in 154/155, is now used extensively. It serves to reduce *b* to three notes and give it a new rhythmical pattern, and it also allows the bass to be heard more easily.

The upper parts immediately break up and are eventually exhausted at 168^1. The fourths have been revived in 166 ff. and these herald the new development of double diminution and shortening of the Subject material.

166^1–174^1.—As Tovey remarks★, the fugue has hitherto been vocal in style, with no prospect of developing into any climax characteristic of the pianoforte. The double diminution solves this problem so that the music seems to burst into flame. The growth continues, helped by a general resumption of playing *tutte le corde*.

The omission of the third and fourth notes enables the double diminution to be accommodated in a half-bar. It retains all the necessary characteristics of the Subject; a full statement would have been fussy. The main aim is now to get a succession of semiquavers to lead into the Final Section. The double diminutions are shared among all parts (intervals are again occasion-

★ *A Companion to Beethoven's Pianoforte Sonatas*, pp. 285 f.

ally altered), and they form an effective link until the entry in 170^2 ff.

At 170^2 the middle part introduces the Subject again in inversion, but in the original note-lengths, with the intervals of *a* slightly widened. What Beethoven wrote should be compared with the normal form:

Ex. 88 (a)

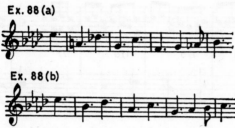

Ex. 88 (b)

By an adroit change at 170^1, the double diminution is made to begin on the accent in the middle part and to be in close *stretto* with the soprano. This new position of the motif is maintained as the music fuses into the Final Section at 174^2. The bass motifs in 171–173 repeat their lowest notes, the technique to be used in 175 ff., which gives the effect of a held note. The speed was reduced at 168 for the double diminutions to be appreciated as such. When these are sufficiently established the *tempo* quickens to the original speed from 174^2. There is thus a sense of *accelerando* from quavers to slow semiquavers and then to fast semiquavers. More important, however, is the fact that the bass motifs of 171–173 are not really diminutions, but a melodic way of writing:

Ex. 89

There is now every need of returning to the traditional speed, because the Final Section uses extensively this vibrating form of harmony and is also in some respects a recapitulation of the opening bars of the first section of the fugue.

It should be noted how concentrated is the Middle Section. In every bar the Subject is heard in some form. No episodes disturb the continuous growth of the music and their omission is a definite part of Beethoven's scheme.

Final Section (174^2–213^1)

174^2–188^1.—Now that the implications of the figuration are clear, the Final Section is heard to begin as follows:

Ex. 90.

The first three entries are announced in the same key, in the same forms, and by the same voices as at the opening of the fugue. By doing so, Beethoven reconciles the fugue with the usual claim of sonata style, that of recapitulation, but this he varies. Here now is polyphony with a homophonic appearance and an instrumental setting as the music moves now towards a pianistic climax.

The middle part moves unobtrusively in canon with the bass, while the upper part adopts the usual tied and untied quaver movement of the Countersubject.

The Answer in 178^2 ff. remains the lowest part, so that Beethoven ingeniously introduces a feeling of four parts while only three sound at once. Again the upper parts are like the Countersubject in style. A codetta, almost exactly similar to that in 34^2–36^1, precedes the third entry at 184^2.

More concessions are made to homophony; four parts are more strongly felt, though often only three are necessary:

Ex. 91

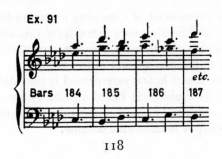

because much of the fourth part is a completion of the harmony, *arpeggiando*. The decoration of the bass in 184^2 and 186^1 is so contrived as to suggest the double diminutions. The introduction of extra crotchet-quaver movement (186^2 f.) prevents the stodginess that may otherwise be felt.

188^2–200^1.—A section in the manner of an episode follows, which recapitulates the rising sequence of 66^2–72^1. The music rises ever higher with joyful abandon, and is extended to four statements of *b*, rejoicing as they go towards the dramatic chord of the diminished seventh at 194^2. Again there are occasionally four essential parts.

From 196^2 the music descends in order to inaugurate a final tonic pedal. A cadence which a lesser composer might have extended to:

Ex. 92

with possibly a repetition of the final chord to begin the entry, Beethoven contracts into half a bar. As a result the Subject can begin on the last chord of the cadence (200^2).

200^2–213^1.—Counterpoint at last gives way. A final entry of the Subject appears, fully harmonized and extended by a bar. The pedal remains as the last link with the fugue, which ends virtually at 200^2. The claims of the sonata style prevail for this coda and make the movement end in a dramatic flourish. Perhaps also, the harmonic style of counterpoint as at 53–56 and 62–65, where the Countersubject and the 'free' part run parallel and each follows the outline of the Subject, foreshadows this present fully homophonic setting.

The end of the Subject turns upwards in 205, so that a rising sequence is evolved in 206–209^1. Almost the entire compass of Beethoven's pianoforte has now been reached, and the large gap between the hands is filled in by the final chord in extended arpeggios to the end, which resembles the similar passage at the end of the Exposition (110^2–114^1).

So very thrilling is the striving upward of 200^2–209^1 and so very occupied with spiritual matters was Beethoven at this time, that one is tempted to put emotion above reason, and wonder if he intended any symbolic illustration here. We shall never know. At all events, this passage carries out the aspiring nature of the Subject to its logical and inevitable conclusion, which satisfies our strongest musical demands.

VIII

VARIATION XXXII, THIRTY-THREE VARIATIONS ON A WALTZ OF DIABELLI, OP. 120 (1823)

Principal Editions:

1. *Gesamtausgabe*, XVII, 64–7 (Nr. 165).
2. Adolf Ruthardt, ed., *Variationen für Klavier zu 2 Händen*, I, 59–62.

T̲HE Diabelli Variations, in which set this great fugue appears, were written after the last sonatas, between 1819 and 1823. Originally, Diabelli had written a Waltz and invited fifty-one of the most prominent composers and performers in contemporary Austria to contribute one variation each. The fifty-one included Schubert, Czerny, Hummel, the boy Liszt, and Beethoven. Some were slow to submit their variation, and the collection took a number of years to complete. Beethoven, on the other hand, soon decided to write not merely one, but a set of variations. When Diabelli realized this he arranged to make two publications, one being devoted to Beethoven's set and the other to the combined work of the remaining fifty musicians. The Diabelli Variations finally appeared in June 1823.

The work shows Beethoven's continued interest in counterpoint and fugue, which was to be maintained later in such works as the Mass in D, the Ninth Symphony, and the late Quartets, especially the Quartet in C sharp minor, Op. 131 and the

Grosse Fuge, Op. 133. During the course of the Diabelli set, a number of variations show contrapuntal tendencies in varying degrees, the most outstanding being Variation XIX, which is predominantly canonical, and Variation XXIV, which is labelled Fughetta. Variations XXIX, XXX, and XXXI give the effect of a slow movement, as in a sonata. Variation XXXI, which precedes the fugue to be discussed now, is highly ornate and occupies a very similar position to Variation XV of the Fifteen Variations with Fugue, Op. 35. Again, the fugue appears at the culminating point of the whole work and out of its epic music there follows, by a remarkable enharmonic change, a quiet and gracious minuet, Variation XXXIII, in which is incorporated a final coda.

The Sketches

Apart from a few paragraphs of a general nature in the writings of Friedland,[*] Parry,[†] Tovey,[‡] Bekker,[§] and Müller-Blattau,[‖] the only source of historical worth regarding the Diabelli Variations is by Nottebohm,[¶] who deals cursorily with the sketches for the whole work but including, as far as concerns the fugue, only the Subject.

Nottebohm says[**] that sketches for this work are found in diverse places and mostly on loose sheets and leaves and, as Albert Levinsohn has shown[††] how easy and dangerous it is to draw completely false conclusions about the chronology of sketches appearing in such a state, one cannot be certain of their order. However, Nottebohm separates the first sketch

---

[*] M. Friedland, *Zeitstil und Persönlichkeitsstil in den Variationwerken der Musikalischen Romantik*, Inaugural Dissertation, 1930, p. 34.

[†] C. H. H. Parry, 'Variations', *Grove's Dictionary of Music and Musicians*, 5th edn. (ed. Eric Blom), 1954, VIII, 683 f.

[‡] D. F. Tovey, *Beethoven*, 1944, pp. 125–7, 129.

[§] P. Bekker, *Beethoven*, 1925, pp. 142 f.

[‖] J. Müller-Blattau, 'Beethoven und die Variation', *Neues Beethoven-Jahrbuch*, V (1933), 126 ff. Variation XXXII is discussed on pp. 133 f.

[¶] G. Nottebohm, 'Skizzen zu den Variationen Op. 120', *Zweite Beethoveniana*, pp. 568 ff.

[**] Ibid., p. 568.

[††] 'Die Entstehungszeit der Ouverture zu Leonore Nr. 1 Op. 138, mit anschliessenden kritischen Bemerkungen zu Nottebohm's Beethoveniana', *Vierteljahrsschrift für Musikwissenschaft*, IX (1893), 163 ff.

(Ex. 93) from the rest in date, largely, one suspects, because the opening of an early variation (III) occurs next to it; the date he assigns is towards the end of 1822.*

Ex. 93

The remainder, Nottebohm asserts,† show the work near the close and are as follow:

Ex. 94

Later,* he writes that sketches for the 3rd, 4th, 9th, and 10th variations belong to the sketches quoted in Ex. 94. The sketch reproduced in Ex. 93 may not then be very much separated in time from the rest after all. It is impossible to be more precise if, indeed, one can even accept Nottebohm's views. Even so, it seems clear that Beethoven was thinking of Variation XXXIII at the same time as the fugue. The words *letzte Menuet* must mean that this variation was to be the last of the set, and therefore, even then, that Beethoven was probably conceiving the fugue as the last but one.

These sketches show an extraordinary certainty in Beethoven's mind regarding the features of both Subjects of this double fugue. Almost always a descending leap is followed by repeated notes and hesitating drops of a second. If, with Nottebohm, one regards Ex. 93 as Beethoven's first attempt at establishing the material of the fugue, then it seems that he originally conceived it as a fugue on a single subject. Beethoven's marking *Vielleicht so anfangen* ('perhaps beginning thus') may reflect his doubt whether it should be a single or double fugue, but more likely it means uncertainty about the theme itself. He may have thought the opening fifth was too great a divergence from the character of the Waltz. A fourth opens the Waltz and most of the variations. The second sketch reverses the opening with a fourth from tonic to dominant to accord with precedent. The fugue is the only variation outside the key of C major or minor, and a close adherence of the Subject to the Waltz is necessary in order to maintain the stylistic unity of the work.

Subject II appears in the second sketch and causes a change in the latter half of Subject I, which now emphasizes the repeated crotchets better. The marking p in Subject I shows that Subject II is more important, and may account for its original setting above Subject I. The other dynamics sf and f support this and suggest the emphasis of the resolutions rather than the discords, though only the removal of rigid accentuation of each first beat is achieved by this. These markings are not kept in the final version, however.

That Beethoven had the variation of 117^2 ff. in mind is evident from the sketches. Three of them have the characteristic

* p. 572.

quaver movement to accompany Subject I, and the last sketch is an augmentation of the sketch in $\frac{12}{8}$ time. The scales in the first two of these sketches are probably not meant to be variations of Subject II, though the drop through a fifth which opens the sketch marked *Presto* links it with Subject I. These scales have the typical mediocrity of many of Beethoven's first ideas, and he improves them later.

In the sketch in $\frac{12}{8}$ time the scales are more controlled and the shape of Subject II can be traced a little more closely:

Ex. 95

The outline of dropping fifths and rising fourths is a familiar feature of the first part of the fugue* (23 f., bass; 36^4–38^4, alto; 83^4–85^1, soprano (incidental); 94 f., tenor). It is really the widened outline of the original Subject II. The lower mordents that are introduced in this sketch have their origin in the soprano of 5 ff.:

Ex. 96

The last two sketches are a distinct improvement on the preceding two, and would have proved quite adequate. But Beethoven achieves a further improvement. The final version of the new Subject I (here referred to as Ia) at 117^2 ff. reaches a mean between the old Subject I and the new form suggested in the last two sketches. The repeated crotchets are not entirely dispensed with, but convert the plain, equal notes of the sketches into a rhythm. The new rhythm is in effect a dotted rhythm, which is foreshadowed in the bass of 23 f. More than

* Though, of course, there are only two minim beats (or even one semibreve beat) in a bar in this fugue, four crotchet beats are assumed for greater clarity in giving bar and beat numbers.

three statements of this rhythm would have been trite and Beethoven avoids this with the return of the main beat to the beginning of the bar at 120.

Scales are largely abandoned in favour of turns for the final version of the new Subject II (referred to as IIa), but it still follows Subject II closely:

Ex. 97

This Subject is extended backwards for a bar (117^3–118^2), which is necessary in order to support the sustained, soft notes of Subject Ia. These extra quavers are not new, but are based on the soprano in 6 and 5 respectively.

In composing this passage, Beethoven was probably aware first of the need to accompany Subject I fully; then the decision to use material from the codetta for this accompaniment would lead to using it for Subject II also, which might have affected the style of Subject I. The principle of variation is carried still further; the new Subject Ia is less active than the original one, whereas the new Subject IIa is decidedly busier than its counterpart.

The Fugue

Exposition (^{4}/1–28^3)

^{4}/1–6^3.—Three motifs combine to make up the two Subjects: *a* drops a fourth and hammers out the lower note for two bars; *b* is obviously derived from *a* with a drop of a second on the accent and the lower note repeated for the remainder of the bar; *c* is a perfect foil to *a* and *b* and imparts to them a rhythm and design, its lyrical and chromatic element contrasting well with their impetuosity and diatonic movement:

Ex. 98

Of the ten repeated crotchets in the first four bars of the Waltz, nine appear in Subject I, also preceded by a drop of a fourth. A comparison of *b* with the opening of Variation III shows the derivation of the dropping seconds. Subject II is also related to the Waltz. The outline of *c* corresponds to the opening of the Waltz, including the acciaccatura:

Ex. 99

Subject II

Waltz

From the E flat at 4^3, the initial third in *c* is filled in, so that all four notes of the opening of the Waltz may loosely be said to appear in this codetta. By inverting the Subjects (cf. the first sketch in Ex. 94) Beethoven probably thought that the discords resolving inwards would be stronger than if resolved outwards, and though they inevitably appear in inversion during the fugue, the manner of their first presentation always creates the greatest impression.

6^4–14^3.—The continuation of the alto from 6^3 is neatly devised. There is a free inversion of *c* and a diminution of 4^3–6^2:

Ex. 100

c inverted

4^2-6^1 diminished

Both Subjects use sequence freely, which is a great feature of the Waltz, especially in bars 8^3–13^1. The dropping seconds of *b*

127

hint at the conjunct movement of the codetta (5 f.) and the first part of the Countersubject (7 f.), which contrasts distinctly with *a*.

Answer II is placed above Answer I, giving much of the effect of the second sketch. The Countersubject (soprano) runs sequentially with the Answers in 9 f. and begins these bars with falling minor seconds which match the rising semitones of Answer II and emphasize its chromaticism. The G flat of 9^1 sounds all the more inevitable by its absence from the chord in 8^{3-4}. This imparts more weight to the dissonance at 9^1, and similarly at 10^1 and 11^1, thus driving the music along in a grand, sweeping rhythm of one in a bar, which is the best way to consider this fugue. This also clarifies the decorated resolutions of 3 f. and all similar bars. Likewise, the E flat is absent from 10^{3-4}, so that there is not an implied $\frac{6}{4}$ chord but the second inversion ($\frac{4}{3}$) of a secondary seventh chord. The E flat actually heard at 10^2 helps to create the aural illusion.

The codetta of 11 ff. reproduces in the bass the codetta of 5 f., and 12 is continued upwards in sequence, with the soprano in attendance a tenth above, another example of the parallel writing taught by Fux and Albrechtsberger. While the tenor remains on an inner pedal of B flat the alto adds a little motif based on a rising sequence of thirds following the example of the tenor in 11 f. In effect, there are still only three parts.

14^4–20^3.—The entry of Subject I in the tenor gives a significance to the tenor pedal during the codetta. It is in fact anticipating Subject I. Again, tenor and bass share the Subjects, but with Subject I uppermost, as in the opening bars, and the soprano has the Countersubject. Many a lesser composer would have been content to reproduce the Countersubject in 15 ff. exactly as before, as follows:

Ex. 101

By now, such a composer would probably be writing in all four parts. By alternating the two lower parts (cf. 6⁴ ff.), Beethoven secures the effect of a third entry without complicating the texture. In view of the length of the fugue, which Beethoven must already have envisaged, the delay in introducing four-part writing is prudent; in addition, the two Subjects have more chance of becoming familiar to the listener. A rigid adherence to the Countersubject would have over-emphasized the chromatic element, and detracted from the power of the Subjects. More particularly, chromaticisms and distant modulations pervade many of the previous variations, and it is better that this fugue should now largely concentrate on accentuating the more diatonic nature of the Waltz, especially as the fugue itself is in only a related key. Beethoven realizes, however, the importance of maintaining a recognizable semblance of the Countersubject. By expanding the interval from a fourth to a sixth, he provides a new high point in the soprano at 17³. The sixth, hitherto heard harmonically (cf. 6¹,³, soprano and alto, and 8, tenor and bass), now appears melodically for the first time.

20⁴–28³.—Answer I enters in the alto and Answer II seems to steal in almost unawares as part of the soprano's continuous melodic stream, without any preparatory rest. It is effective because, as an upper part, it is heard most distinctly. Even now there are only three real parts, because of parallel thirds (20²–22³, tenor and bass, and 23 f., alto and tenor) and sixths (25, alto and tenor). The Countersubject is entirely absent, and the sequential movement in all parts (23 f.) suggests an episode, though the Exposition is still in progress. The falling fifths in those bars in the bass reflect the opening of Answer I.

A number of elements already heard are fused into the cadential bars (25 ff.) which complete the Exposition. The soprano and alto emphasize the tie over the barline and the resultant syncopation (cf. 6⁴/7¹). The tenor uses the little sequential figure previously heard in the alto of 13^2–15^2, and the bass repeats the familiar B flat pedal, adding the soprano codetta of 5^2–7^2. The bass (27^2–29^2) keeps the movement going during the cadence, giving point also to the entry in the soprano at 28^4.

Episode

28^4–34^3.—This shows great economy of material. It consists exclusively of two-bar sequences based on *a*, with three of the crotchets tied into a dotted minim. As has already been noticed, the Subjects lend themselves easily to sequential treatment. The tenor imitates the soprano at a bar's distance, easily obtaining the effect of *stretto*. The alto states a form of Subject II, which is ingeniously related to both soprano and tenor. The A flat at 30 enters rhythmically to correspond to the soprano entry, but not at the right pitch for Subject II, which would be C. A C is present in the tenor. However, the A flat is at the right pitch to correspond to the tenor entry. For this, of course, it is a bar too soon, but the A flat is prolonged through two bars instead of one before following its course. The third appearance of the sequence in the soprano at 32^4 seems to lessen the force of the bass entry at 34^4. Beethoven is careful to ensure its power in a number of ways. It is clearly separated from the rest of the texture and the left hand can give full weight to stating Subject I. Further, the tenor in 29^4 ff. provides the bass which, with inevitability, leads chromatically downward to the G.

First Middle Section (34^4–63^3)

34^4–44^3.—The primary function of this fugue is to be a variation. A strong reference to the tonality of C helps to identify it with the Waltz before it diverges in key later, to an extent commensurate with its magnitude. By being in C minor three later entries (at 44^4, 55^4, and 57^4) give the essential opening of the Waltz, namely, a C followed by repeated G's. A pedant may not approve the separate harmonization of each crotchet since the minim is the beat. The harmonic progression of the first half of the bar is, however, repeated note for note in the second half. The progression serves to emphasize the new key of C minor and is bound into a whole by the pedal C in the bass entry.

The first entries of this section are now heard widely separated, not in adjacent parts as before. This new scoring is fresh, though it arises originally from artistic necessity. Though the Subjects cannot be altered out of immediate recognition during the fugue like the Waltz theme in the variations, Beethoven does seem to begin here a set of variations in the scoring of the Subjects, which continues through the fugue. The texture is still confined to three real parts, with the free part inside, in the alto. At first sight the material of the alto at 36^4 ff. appears to be new, but it is really a variation on the Countersubject. It reproduces the latter's contour of dropping fifths and rising fourths. This sequence of intervals has also been heard on a more extended scale in the Episode, but it is now in syncopated form, a procedure derived from 26 ff. This, in turn, was derived from $12-17^1$ and originally from $6^4/7^1$. Answer II now fits excellently into the context of C minor, whereas the identical notes in the Episode (30–33, alto) more nearly correspond to E flat. Answer II is cleverly dovetailed at 36 because c is an augmented inversion of 35 f.:

Ex. 102
Bars   35   36   37

Answer I, instead of following the descending melodic minor scale in 37 ff., as would justifiably have occurred in a lesser composer's work, now falls in semitones, emphasizing chromaticism more, and the tenor part in the Episode is now seen to have foreshadowed the bass entry.

A codetta leads to the next entry and is also sequential. All parts follow the bass of 39^2 f., based on the soprano of $5-6^1$ with dropping fifths in the alto which refer to Subject I. Wherever the same note occurs on both sides of the barline, the tie is used, a practice which originated in $6^4/7^1$. Also, the elongation of the alto figure of 13^2-15^2 in the soprano of 42^2-46^1 points to the need for a tie between the B flats at $42^4/43^1$.

44^4-55^3.—The Subjects are now reversed in their respective importance. Answer I enters in an inner part quite unobtrusively, especially as the bass merges into it. Subject II is the more inevitable and effective because 45 f., viewed as a whole, form a strong perfect cadence, in which the bass C at 46 follows naturally from the tenor G's in 45. Tenor and bass here form a continuous bass line. A lesser composer would have been content to reproduce Subject II at its original interval from Subject I and begin on E flat instead of C. The resultant use of a $\frac{6}{3}$ chord would have weakened the C minor tonality, whereas Beethoven wishes to establish this key again more firmly after leaving it in the codetta. In addition, there would have been a superfluity of E flats. At its present pitch, Subject II relates exactly to the alto in 46 ff. This parallel motion is therefore both necessary and relevant, and another variation in the scoring of the fugue themes is obtained. Beethoven accompanies Subject I in sixths and this lack of independence of the parts again makes for clarity of texture without sacrifice of sonority.

The last bar of each Subject carries the music down (49 f.), the better to rise over a G pedal to the next entry at 55^4. This codetta is composed of some elements heard before: the bass pedal of 51 ff. is familiar from $25-27^1$ and 12^3-14^3, and the alto and tenor figure in sequence, originally almost unnoticed in the alto of 13^2-15^2, now becomes more important. The soprano at 49^3 begins with syncopation which recalls the tenor of 12^3-14^3 and, in 51–54, compresses into one-bar motifs the essential shape of Subject I, which provides a fine metamorphosis of this Subject:

Ex. 103

Beethoven could have followed the sequence in the tenor exactly, and then dropped a diminished fifth in both tenor and bass:

Ex. 104

The high-pitched entries at 55^4 ff. would not then have sounded so natural and logical after the depths of 46–53. The octaves between tenor and bass achieve this perfectly. This problem of balance gives variety to the opening of *a*, which now becomes a diminished seventh. The music is ignited by this dramatic move and returns to the lightness of three parts, to which the leap in the bass at 54^4 gives still more spring. The leap of a seventh is put to further use by being part of a cadence; the thought in 53^1–55^1 is:

Ex. 105

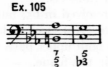

55^4–63^3.—The third entries of the Middle Section appear now after their masterly preparation. These bars show great craftsmanship. A higher register is used not only to contrast with 46–53, but also to throw the bass entry at 63^4 into the strongest possible relief. It is now the turn of Subject II to be accompanied (in thirds), so that it is now heard simultaneously at its usual position (alto) in relation to Subject I and at the new level a third lower (tenor), first used in the bass in 46 ff. Soprano and bass have Subject I in *stretto* and so form a continuous pedal over four bars, which subtly extends the pedal device already used.

All four parts are now devoted to stressing the Subjects, and Subject I is carried through to include the conjunct movement of the original codetta of 5–6^3 in both soprano and bass. This pursuance of the *stretto* (60 ff.), and the parallel movement of tenor and bass (62 f.), reinforced by adding the soprano in 63, enhance the *legato* motion, hitherto undeveloped. The progression C–F in the soprano ($61^4/62^1$) lightly hints at the inversion of Subject I and is placed at the same rhythmical point as the beginning of *a*. With the preceding G (61^3), this progression has been heard before, in the soprano of 32^4–34, which recalls the bass of 23 f., the tenor of 29^4–31^4, and the alto of 36^4–38. The subsequent inversions grow logically therefore out of the earlier music.

Second Middle Section in Inversion

63^4–67.—Subject I is prominent in every way; it is in octaves for the first time, a procedure hinted at in 53^4 f., and its register, dynamics, distance from the upper parts, and the very fact of inversion, all emphasize it greatly. The free part (alto) uses the newly established conjunct movement and abandons sequence, now so well developed. Its somewhat inconsequential chromaticisms recall the first part of the original Counter-subject in the soprano of 7 f., though now it follows more closely the rising of the Subjects.

The discord is not resolved in 65, but this is not perceived aurally on account of the great speed of the fugue. The dropping fifth which appears in both upper parts has, moreover, a very powerful connotation in this fugue.

Beethoven shows a fine sense in the balance of keys here. The Middle Section in C minor was very extended in order to establish the relation with the key of the Waltz. All other keys through which he passes are to be treated transitorily, just as were the hints at various keys in the Waltz. Therefore, only one entry is given to F minor (63^4 f.) and the music modulates immediately. Only C minor and E flat major are allowed to play a large part.

Episode (68–85^3)

68–79^3.—Beethoven maintains constant variety in this fugue. He changes from the usual short Episodes of four or six bars and embarks on a long one instead. A transitional passage (68 ff.) based on the conjunct movement of the original codetta is followed by an apparent Middle Section in D flat at 71^4, but after *a*, *b* is somewhat transformed, so that there is really a variation of Subject I or, strictly speaking, Answer I:

134

Ex.106

The bass enters in *stretto* two bars later, as if echoing its entry in the second Middle Section, but only with *a*.

In a long Episode, Beethoven could have written less concentratedly than at other points in the fugue. This Episode however is more concentrated than ever. In the alto and tenor, *c* is, in effect, advanced a whole bar, though this is not immediately apparent because the first note is shortened to a minim. This puts the two Subjects in a slightly different relationship. The inversion of *a* in the bass also has its companion in the tenor of 74^3–75^3, which enriches the texture greatly like the low notes of the viola in a string quartet. The two lower parts have not been placed together in a low register since 62, and they come freshly on the ear at this point. Beethoven never forgets that he is primarily writing a variation, and it is not fanciful to regard 71^4 ff. as a variation of bars 8–13 of the Waltz:

Ex. 107

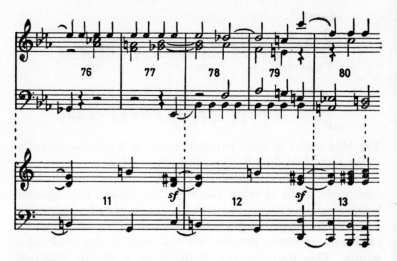

Considered in this way, the contrary motion of the outer parts in the Waltz accounts for the inversion of the bass in the fugue, and the separation by two bars of the inversion from the normal version reflects the Waltz's repeated motif.

79⁴–85³.—The syncopation in 80 ff. sets up a conflict. The coincidence of the fourth crotchets in the alto of 80–82 with the first note of *a*, now shortened to a bar, strengthens the syncopation, but, taken as a whole, 80–83 follow the normal accentuation. From 84² to 85³ Beethoven has marked *sforzandi* which show that the prominent feature is syncopation. The progression preceding these *sforzandi* (83⁴/84¹) is not marked *sf.* These two chords form a pivot, during which the beat is changed from adherence to the barline to syncopation. The whole Episode is an excellent example of a combination of artistry and craftsmanship and ends in C minor with *a* reduced to a half-bar and finally extinguished.

Final Section of First Part (85⁴–117¹)

85⁴–95³.—Subject I enters (alto) in the original key and the juxtaposition with C minor sounds quite natural. The entry is disguised cleverly and eliminates a feeling of finality resulting from the return to the tonic, which is not properly established until 89. The ever-descending soprano of 85² f. draws attention from the alto entry, and only the dramatic leap of a ninth to

136

begin Subject II separates this section aurally from the Episode. The bass follows Subject II rhythmically, to which it bears much the same relation as in 23 f. Incidentally, the dropping fifths have not been presented in minims on the beat before (cf. syncopations in the alto of 37^2 f.), and the beat needs now to be emphasized after the foregoing Episode. The acciaccatura E natural (87^1, soprano) is the only ornament in the fugue. It causes the hand to roll right over and give full weight to the entry of Subject II, which might otherwise be played weakly, though the music is marked *piano*. Hitherto this marking has appeared for only two or three bars (25 ff.). In the tenor at 89^3, Beethoven has to use the dominant to avoid three E flats in the chord.

During the fugue Subject II is often stated in thirds. In 91 ff. the scoring is varied from close thirds to a distance of two octaves and a third (soprano and bass). The entry of the soprano at 91 is really a continuation of the alto of 90, so that this melodic line is clearly derived from the soprano of 5 f. It is also a stroke of artistic genius. Beethoven decorates the B flat with an inverted turn, and so avoids complete stagnation. As the only moving part, it illuminates this bar, which, together with 92, gives one of the most emotional moments of the entire fugue. In terms of Subject II, 5^4–7 take on added significance:

Ex. 108

The different rhythmical placing in the bar also gives this motif freshness.

The bass from 93^2 provides a hint of the inversion in 95^4 ff., which is very reminiscent of the anticipation in the soprano at 61^4 of the other entry in inversion. The bass of 93^4 ff. also continues the alto an octave lower.

95^4–105^3.—Both Subjects use sequence in their construction and lend themselves to sequential extension, which has been used a little in 49–54, but now dominates the music and shows

Beethoven's mastery. Subject I enters, as at 63^4, in inversion and octaves, *fortissimo*. The inverted *b* is continued in upward sequence for no less than seven bars. The tenor reinforces it in sixths for over three bars from 102 and adds to the energy. Eventually, the soprano enters at 105^4 and cuts the sequence short. The tenor's upward octave leap at 105^3 is a practical consideration for the pianist, so that he can secure a firm entry in the soprano.

The alto in 97 might well have been a semibreve D natural, but a chromatic change is made which echoes that of the previous bar. This bar (96) is itself the inversion of part of the Countersubject (8, soprano). Inversion is now the characteristic of the music.

Subject II is reduced to one statement of *c*, which is also treated sequentially. By overlapping this motif in alto and tenor, one is aware only of a succession of rising thirds. This overlapping is implicit in Subject II (see Ex. 98). The rising thirds also reflect the little alto motif of 13^2–15^2 which has been alluded to before. At 105^3–106^4 the identical notes of this motif are used in a contracted form, and give the original motif a significance one would scarcely have forecast for it.

105^4–117^1.—Subject I is now metamorphosed. A variation of the fugue is to follow at 117^2 and the original form of the Subject will not be wanted. Subject I starts normally with *a*, *recto*, but *b* is then caught in the upward surge and rises to a high peak at 111^4. Subject I in the bass of 108 ff. shows *a* decapitated, followed by *b*, and then it breaks off. The alto and tenor of 107 ff. attempt Subject II, and the tenor is nearly successful. The bass repeats the leap of a diminished seventh at $111^4/112^1$, heard in $53^4/54^1$, so that the high point of the fugue has the chord of the diminished seventh. It is effective here because it has previously been used judiciously and sparingly. The chord pervades the music until the pause at 117^1. The large gap between the hands in 112^4 ff. is characteristic of Beethoven, and gives prominence and effectiveness to the alto and tenor in 112^4–113^3. Beethoven could, at this point, have led straight into Variation XXXIII, for at 160 it is from this same chord of the diminished seventh, over the tonic E flat, that he eventually moves to the *letzte Menuet*. But he can still do something outstanding with his material.

Variation of the Fugue (117²–160)

117²–125¹.—In the spirit of Variation, the fundamental purpose of this work, Beethoven now constructs a sort of Variation within a Variation. The new forms of the Subjects (Ia and IIa) are again treated fugally, though the new section is not extended to great lengths. The reappearance of Subject I in its original form at 142 and Subject II at 147 finally establishes in the mind that this section is a variation of the first 117 bars. The new section sounds so fresh also because, from 102 to the pause, Beethoven has almost obliterated the contrapuntal aspect of the music and substituted a solidly harmonic setting. Now the counterpoint returns.

After the first statement of the Subjects, the codetta appears, now abbreviated to one bar, though it maintains its characteristic turn. Then the same three parts (soprano, tenor, and bass) as were heard together in 8 ff. are heard together again in 121–124. This time, the soprano has Answer IIa and the tenor anticipates the bass rhythmically in *stretto* and its first note is provided by the A flat in the soprano at 120⁴. This alternation of beat between tenor and bass is very similar to that between the alto and tenor (and bass) in 80 ff.

Beethoven deliberately writes a ⁶₄ chord in 122, followed by an open fifth at 123¹, which is emphasized by doubling the B flat in the tenor. This is not necessarily carelessness. The pedal nature of Subject I, and hence of Subject Ia, is stressed by this break with 'good fugal writing'. Therefore at 121³, the tenor becomes the real bass, and it combines satisfactorily with the soprano in this and the next bar. Any objection in 123 is short lived because the movement is too rapid for the ear to realize it, and the harmonic bass has returned to the bass part.

In the codetta (124²–125¹), the repeated A flats and B flats in the soprano maintain the pedal device prominently, whereas the passage may well have read:

Ex. 109

This would have been a mechanical repetition of 120, allowing for the inversion of the two parts, and a third hearing of it at 132 would have been tedious.

125^2–132^1.—Alto and bass provide the third entry and the soprano assumes the tenor's role. The soprano now echoes Subject Ia in *stretto*, instead of leading it, and breaks off at 128^1 to accompany the alto in the codetta. The scales used in the sketches seem now to find an outlet in the free bass of 128–130^1.

The entries at 129^2 ff. make another variation. The Answer, which normally begins with a drop of a fifth, now begins with a fourth. As a result, the music undergoes a flattening of the tonality, which recalls a similar flattening in bars 28 ff. of the Finale *Alla Fuga* in the Fifteen Variations with Fugue, Op. 35. A sudden modulation to A flat occurs in $129^{1/2}$ and the alto D flat (129^3) confirms the key for this entry. These new tonal surroundings prepare the listener for the entry in F minor at 135^2. Subject II also appears in slightly different shape. It is altered in 130^{3-4} because the original shape of these quavers (C, B flat, A flat, A natural) would have caused too much conflict with the A natural at 130^1, and made the music in general and the alto in particular too uncertain and vague. Accordingly, a little of the vibrating motif of the codetta at 120 is substituted at $130^{3, 4}$, which brings this aspect into greater prominence. The bass is also varied in 130^3 f., reversing the order of the falling fifth and rising fourth, by putting the B flat at 131^1 an octave higher. In addition, the bass of 131 f. produces a static version of *a* in Answer form, so that the repeated crotchets become a sustained pedal. This emphasizes still further the pedal nature of Subject I, already referred to.

Episode

132^2–135^1.—This is the outcome of extending the familiar codetta with relevant material. The obvious progression at $134^3/135^1$ is as shown in Ex. 110, but this is impracticable in performance as tenor and bass alone would require both hands. By depriving 135^1 of the upper A flat (alto) and the low F (bass), Beethoven prevents any increase of tone that a player may make involuntarily from 132, which would anticipate the *crescendo* at 138.

Ex. 110

Middle Section

135²–141.—Beethoven's ingenuity here is interesting. The tenor represents Subject IIa, and begins at the correct pitch in relation to Subject Ia (135³˒⁴). Continued at this pitch, it would merge with the bass pedal at 136¹, and so is raised a third to the exact pitch of the previous alto entry in 130¹ f. Even the deviation in 130³˒⁴ is retained in 136³˒⁴. The pitch is restored at 138¹ by inverting 137³˒⁴:

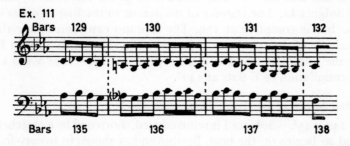

Ex. 111

The alto at 135⁴/136¹ completes the chord of F minor begun by the soprano, so that the whole chord is heard in arpeggio; rhythmically, a *stretto* is felt here but the alto continues by accompanying the tenor. Consecutive octaves occur between soprano and tenor at 137¹ᐟ², but as usual, the listener is not aware of them in the high speed of the music, and they seem only to mock the pedant.

At 138² the alto repeats the previous soprano entry an octave lower. The tenor begins Subject IIa at the same pitch as before, but does not now deviate until 139³ (cf. 129³ f., alto). In all these variations of Subject IIa, the quaver movement is the unifying feature which makes them aurally acceptable.

The tone of the bass F pedal in 135 ff. gradually diminishes, so that the tenor, always the musical bass in these bars, becomes the actual bass quite naturally at 138, without the listener's being aware of what has happened. The merging of Subject Ia into the soprano in 138 ff. to make one continuous descent is also noteworthy. Beethoven could easily have composed 137 f. as follows:

Ex. 112

This would have been much less artistic. The accent would suddenly have been brought to the first beat of the bar. As it is, the A flat minim at $138^{2,3}$ advances the accent to the second crotchet and for a fleeting moment stops the incessant rhythm of Subject Ia. The transfer of the accent to the first crotchet of the bar is complete at 139. The soprano can then follow the example of the tenor in 121 ff. and be in *stretto* with Subject Ia in the alto. The tied F's in the soprano at $141^4/142^1$ avoid an accumulation of E flats at 142^1.

Final Section of the Whole Fugue (142–160)

$142–145^3$.—Subject I is reintroduced, shortened by a crotchet, and so begins on the beat. Beethoven has shown in twenty-five bars (117–141) that the varied two Subjects are fruitful enough for another double fugue, but he has determined not to become enmeshed any further in developing the material. Instead, he is concerned with winding up the fugue by recapitulating the original forms of the Subjects to keep the size of the fugue in check. Variation XXXII cannot therefore be considered as two fugues.

However, the old material is not recapitulated too suddenly. The reappearance of Subject I has been carefully prepared, but Subject II is delayed until after the next entry of Subject I at 145^4. In its place, Subject I is heard with the original form of Subject IIa. The latter fits perfectly and, moreover, proves its derivation from Subject II. The return to the normal form of Subject IIa is more effective because of the recent deviations from it in 130^{3,4}, 136 f., and 139^3–140^1. The familiar vibrating codetta would not have fitted in 145 (cf. 120) because of consecutive fifths, but the two turns which are substituted are familiar in origin (cf. 120, soprano, and 5 f., soprano).

145^4–153^3.—The entry of Subject I again and not Answer I causes the tonic key of E flat to be stressed as the fugue nears its end. Subject II is now recapitulated in 147 ff. This is the first time that they both appear at the same pitch as in Beethoven's sketch (see Ex. 94). Minims, crotchets, and quavers are now linked together more clearly in one texture. There is only a hint of Subject IIa in the bass. Movement in quavers has long become established, and is now used to create more and more excitement for the final climax.

Answer I in the soprano at 149^4 again leans to the subdominant (cf. 129^2 ff., tenor). Here the aim is a more effective foreshadowing of the end of the fugue. Beethoven shows a fine sense of balance in using the subdominant. In 129^2 ff. it was of secondary importance and merely steered the tonality to the entry in F minor at 135^2. Accordingly it was placed in an inside part. Now, it is of fundamental importance, and so appears an octave higher in the soprano, where it can be heard most easily.

153^4–160.—The fugue is not to end in E flat and does not return to it. The music now moves to the chord of the diminished seventh from which it will slip back chromatically to the key of the whole work, C major. For this reason, the subdominant key (A flat) is strengthened in order to efface the tonic key. The D naturals (153, bass) emphasize the suggestion by the E flats in 154 (tenor and bass) of a dominant pedal in the key of A flat. So strong now is the A flat tonality, that Answer I at 153^4 ff. must really be considered as Subject I.

The soprano in 155 ff. outlines Answer II (or Subject II) in the bass. This is the first time that such accompaniment begins on the same note heard simultaneously in Subject I. Here it reinforces the new pedal on the dominant of A flat.

In 157^4 ff. the soprano continues with *b*, which keeps the important D flats before the listener. They appear in almost every bar from 147. The A flat–E flat relationship is preserved to the end, as the bass again presents a static version of a in 157^3 ff. (cf. 131 f.). Finally, the relationship is incorporated into the harmony on the pause in the bass. The alto and tenor meanwhile use the mannerisms of Subject IIa in 158 f. The low pitch of the tenor and its movement in sixths with the alto make the music slow down and stop eventually on the chord of the diminished seventh again. The approach to this chord is different from that used before in 111^4–117^1. Instead of being repeated before the pause, the chord now occurs for the first time on the pause. As a result it still sounds fresh and is not overworked.

After the chord has passed in arpeggio four times through the keyboard, an echo of the opening of Subject Ia is heard three times in a more drawn-out rhythm as the music leads neatly in six bars of *Poco Adagio* back to C major. The tied minim and crotchet of Subject Ia, extended to a tied semibreve and crotchet, makes the anticipatory note still more poignant. The sounds fade away and dissolve imperceptibly into the final variation.

IX
FUGHETTAS, FUGATOS, CANONS,
AND SHORT PASSAGES OF
IMITATIVE WRITING

THE Principal Editions for these extracts remain, of course, the same as for the fugues, but the detailed page references have been omitted in order to facilitate their presentation.

These passages, though much less extended, are often by no means negligible, and in a few cases are intensely moving. They are here arranged in order of composition.

Praeludium in F minor (date uncertain, probably 1785 or 1787): Bars 4, 8^2–10, 24–27^2

This short piece, though for pianoforte, appears more suitable for the organ (manuals only), and seems a conscious imitation of J. S. Bach's organ works, some of which Beethoven may have come to know as a result of his teacher Neefe's being then the court organist at Bonn.

After the opening three bars the music settles down into three voices. At 4^1 the alto initiates a point imitated at the octave by soprano and bass at a minim's distance. The continuation by the soprano makes a surprising foreshadowing of the main theme of the third movement of the Sonata in F minor, Op. 57 (*Appassionata*). The fact that the Sonata was composed in 1804 and the Praeludium was published in 1805, together with the use of the same key, suggests a strong connexion between the two works.

The bass at 8^2 begins another set of entries of the same point. Exposed octaves occur between soprano and bass in 9^{1-2} with no compensating benefit. They could easily have been avoided with the added advantage of using the point and giving it a different rhythmical placing, as follows:

Ex. 113

At 24^2 the alto gives a new motif based on the quavers of 1, which the bass takes up more exactly at 25^1. The alto enters again at 26^2 with a slightly altered form of its statement at 24^2. From the spacing of the entries it seems as if Beethoven had originally planned to give the soprano an entry at 25^3, but in the end the soprano does not join in the counterpoint, though its downward scales in 24 and 26 recall the scale in 2.

Twenty-four Variations in D on the Arietta 'Venni amore' by Righini (1790)

(a) *Variation VII*

Sketches for a number of the variations in this set appear in an advanced state in a sketch-book in the British Museum.* In the top right-hand corner of one leaf† Beethoven has written *Orgel Variationen*, but the sketches that follow seem to have no connexion with the organ and sometimes, as in this case, exceed the lower range of a manual. It is possible that Beethoven had originally intended to devote the page to some organ variations but used it for these piano variations instead. Four of the five variations sketched are headed with a number. Where a number is decipherable it does not correspond with the number of the appropriate variation in the final version.

The sketch of Variation VII appears at the top of the page and is given a number that may be 2. There is only one sharp

* Add. MS. 29801.　　† fo. 123 v.

in the key-signature, but two are understood. A well-worn
crease could partly obliterate the C sharp, but there is no trace
of it at all. The sketch is here quoted in full:

Ex. 114

A comparison with the Theme and Variation I shows that
Beethoven was basing this variation very closely on the melodic
outline of the Theme. In the final version, the first bar of both

entries is eliminated, so that the bass opening gives appropriately the impression of being a variation of the bass of the first two bars of the Theme. Beethoven's treatment of the canon in the sketch shows that a texture resulting from widely spaced hands, characteristic of his late music, was already being achieved. The upper part is twice thrown up an octave instead of following the outline set by the bass. This shows the origin of the canon starting two octaves apart and of the top B in bar 3 of the final version. A slight alteration in the bass line leads Beethoven into using suspended sevenths which are a distinct improvement on the sketch, and are continued long enough for bars 5–8 of the sketch to need condensing into three bars in the variation.

In the sketch for the second part of the variation, Beethoven writes thirteen bars of which the fifth to ninth bars inclusive are later cut out. The other major alterations are that the first two bars of the upper part are lowered an octave and the next two bars are similarly raised. This enables the music to make an evenly graded ascent to the final D. Beethoven has also lightly crossed out the E at *. This semiquaver was probably a slip of the pen because he writes a G crotchet elsewhere in the sketch.

In the variation the entry of the alto in 2, two octaves higher than the bass, corresponds to the D in the right hand of bar 2 of the Theme and so the variation can still follow the Theme closely in pitch, despite the lack of the original first bar. The shape of the motif at 3^2 is altered melodically, giving rise to a scale to 5^1, which is adopted in the bass at 4^2. This scale has been taken from bars 5 f. of the sketch.

At 9 the alto announces this scale in a shortened form, which is now seen as the filling-in of the minor seventh in bar 9 of the Theme (bass). Each voice begins on A to preserve the pedal in the Theme, and continues by resolving the dominant seventh chord. Finally, in 14 ff., the soprano extends the scale further, through an octave and a fourth. In thus making further use of a given idea, Beethoven makes the music grow organically from what has gone before, and is already showing himself a master of the variation style of composition. At the last moment the bass inserts a little echo by means of delaying the rise of the bass to the tonic. Long since, the original form of the motif has been abandoned. It was retained only as long as it was useful in outlining the Theme, but the rhythm was retained to give unity to the variation. The staggering of the cadence, with the resultant $^6_4$ chord, is a device frequently met in Beethoven's music, and it is interesting to note this characteristic of his style so early in his output. It may also be seen in some of the other variations in this set.

(b) Variation XIX

This variation begins as a canon, strict as to intervals, but departures from strictness gradually appear. The rhythmical imitation, however, is maintained throughout, except for one short break in 12.

Again, the chief function of the music is to be a variation, and the music is easily seen to be based on the outline of the Theme. At 2^2 the upper part rises an octave, compared with the Theme. This clarifies the texture by keeping the two hands well apart, and makes a more satisfactory answering phrase to the first one.

In 9 ff. the canon has to be abandoned melodically in order that the effect of the two resolutions of the dominant seventh chord can be reproduced. As a result, the second half of the variation is in two halves, the latter being an inversion of the former. 13 and 15, as inversions of 9 and 11, contain fourths, which are incorrectly treated and show Beethoven's imperfect knowledge of double counterpoint before he left Bonn.

(c) Variation XXI, Bars 9–16

In this variation, the pedal effect of the second half of the Theme is transferred to the first half. This provides an opportunity for a contrapuntal treatment of the minor seventh in bar 9 of the Theme (bass). As this interval is part of the dominant seventh chord which resolves in the next bar, it is logical here for tonic to answer dominant. The seventh of the dominant seventh chord has to be answered by an octave. These two forms of the motif stress the resolution.

In 13 the soprano entry cuts across the alto. The clash is ingeniously lightened by shortening the first note and inserting a rest.

149

Twelve Variations on the Minuet à la Vigano, from the Ballet 'Le nozze disturbate' by Haibl (1795)

(a) *Variation XI*

This variation opens canonically, following the outlines of the Theme quite closely. Only the rhythm is strictly imitated, and this breaks off at 3^3. When the imitation is resumed at 12^3, the effect is of three parts in *stretto*, though the music is confined to a play on the opening motif.

(b) *Variation XII, Bars 4^2–8^3, 12^2–16^2*

At 4^2 the music of this variation breaks into a short canon in octaves at two crotchets' distance. The two motifs used are the rising scale and the descending thirds, which are heard from the beginning of the variation. These motifs are of course heard in the Theme. Inspection shows that the canon, which begins at the octave, cannot be continued throughout at that interval because of consecutive fifths at $6^{2/3}$. The position is soon restored. In making this deviation Beethoven is able to use all the material of the first three bars of the variation.

At the resumption of the canon at 12^2, it is reduced to one crotchet's distance, with the upper part leading. Again, the canon is not kept at the octave throughout, as the music follows more closely the course of the Theme at this point.

Sonata in A, Op. 2, No. 2 (1795): 1st Movement, Bars 180–198

Shedlock* gives the following sketch as the origin of this passage from the Development section, though without giving its source:

Ex. 115

* J. S. Shedlock, *Beethoven's Pianoforte Sonatas*, 1918, pp. 37 f.

and suggests that it looks very much as if Beethoven had some intention of writing a movement for strings. It certainly lies uncomfortably under the hands on the keyboard.

The nature of the close imitation at the octave in three parts at a crotchet's distance is the same as in the sketch and is not developed any further. The motif is based on the one heard earlier in the section, in 160^2–162^2, which opens in F major as does the sketch. This traverses two upward octaves and is thus related to the two downward octaves of the main theme. The imitations are completed in two bars and amount to no more than a decorated chord. They are repeated four times to 188^2 to make four different chords. Two more repetitions occur at 191^2 and 196^2.

Sonata in C, Op. 2, No. 3 (1795): 3rd Movement

This Scherzo is opened by three voices in turn enunciating a motif, the melodic shape of whose first four notes is a common feature of the opening of all four movements, and is their unifying factor. The continuation of each entry is by a descending scale (cf. the rising scale in the last movement), with a modification in the second entry, which recalls the first two movements very strongly:

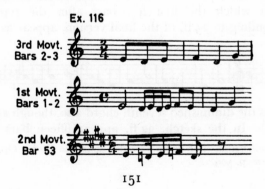

Ex. 116

3rd Movt.
Bars 2-3

1st Movt.
Bars 1-2

2nd Movt.
Bar 53

This modification prevents an open octave at 4^1. Once the entries are made, the counterpoint gives way to harmony.

At 8^2 contrapuntal writing is resumed, with the soprano concentrating on the first four notes and the lower parts stating an extended scale.

At 16^2 the alto begins as at 8^2, but at 21 the voices are interchanged to give the effect of double counterpoint until 27, when the voices merge into one.

The opening section is recapitulated in 39^2 ff., and this time the bass is modified as well. This modification is made with the superficial object of strengthening the C major tonality, but in doing so, Beethoven economizes with his material at the same time.

The middle section is also recapitulated (47^2 ff.) in a free manner without inversion.

Eight Variations on 'Ich hab' ein kleines Hüttchen nur' (? c. 1795): Variation VI

This variation is in two-part counterpoint, each part in octaves throughout. The imitation is not strictly carried out in the first half, though the continuance of the bass by itself in 8 gives the aural impression of being the end of a canon. The second half however is almost canonical in strictness, and begins at a bar's distance, but is reduced to a crotchet's distance to increase the tension. Just then, at 14^2, the canon ends. Beethoven deludes the listener into thinking that this variation is more highly contrapuntal than it is.

Sonata in E flat, Op. 7 (1796): 3rd Movement, Bars 25–32[1]

Nottebohm reproduces* an extended sketch for this movement in which the first few bars after the repeat sign, corresponding to 25 ff. of the final version, appear as follow:

Ex. 117

This uses the diminished seventh chord also, though at a different pitch. In the sketch, 32 ff. appear fifteen bars after the

* G. Nottebohm, 'Der dritte Satz der Sonate in Es-dur Op. 7', *Zweite Beethoveniana*, p. 509.

repeat sign, whereas Beethoven prunes this to seven bars in the final version.

The first two bars of the sketch (Ex. 117) suggest the imitation at the octave which Beethoven maintains. The little canon consists solely of the notes of the diminished seventh chord, and amounts to only a decorative way of sustaining the chord.

Sonata in F, Op. 10, No. 2 (1796–7 or 1798): 3rd Movement

Shedlock reproduces* a sketch for the theme of this movement:

Ex. 118

The E in the fourth bar is shown as lacking a quaver bar across the stem, but this is presumably an accidental omission. The sketch shows that the feature of three repeated notes was fixed before the melodic shape.

The semiquaver motif of 3 f. is an extension and decoration of the drop of a third in 2^2. The answering of tonic with dominant is delayed until the third entry. There is no attempt at a regular fugue style presentation of the material. Beethoven establishes the key of F over two entries before modulating to the dominant. The Answer, if such it can now be called, is irregular in not beginning on F, but Beethoven wishes to stress the new key. Meanwhile, the two lower parts accompany in thirds, as the counterpoint merges into harmony.

At 41 there is an effect of *stretto*, though both parts move in parallel motion. The second half of the theme is given a similar treatment separately (47 ff.).

Eight Variations on the Theme 'Une fièvre brûlante', from the Opera 'Richard Cœur de Lion' by Grétry (1797–8): Variation IV, Bars 16^3–24^1

The motif of this short piece of imitative writing is based on the rising motif of bars 17 ff. of the Theme. The fall of the bass in 19 f. and the soprano in 22^3 ff. may have been suggested by the fall in bar 19 of the Theme.

* 'Beethoven's Sketch Books', *Musical Times*, XXXIII, 462 (1st August 1892).

*Ten Variations on the Theme 'La stessa, la stessissima', from the Opera
'Falstaff' by Salieri (1798): Variation VI*

This variation opens contrapuntally in a confident major to
contradict the minor of the previous variation. Only the rhythm
is exactly the same with each entry, except in 2^1, where the
semiquavers give the quavers their initial impetus. At 5^2 these
semiquavers are augmented to quavers to give a lyrical sweep
to the upper parts.

*Seven Variations on the Quartet 'Kind, willst du ruhig schlafen', from
the Opera 'Das unterbrochene Opferfest' by Winter (1798 or 1799)*

(a) Variation VI, Bars 20^2-23

A short point occurs at 20^2 imitated at the octave below a bar
later. The lower part at 23^1 is a diminution of the upper part in
22. These few bars make a contrapuntal variation of the
corresponding bars in the Theme.

(b) Coda, Bars 36^1-40

At the 36th bar of the Coda, during the section marked
Molto Allegro, appear five bars of canon at the octave at a bar's
distance. This is the natural outcome of the development at
the beginning of the Molto Allegro section, where the music
becomes contrapuntal, with rhythmical imitation. The motif
of the canon comes from these earlier bars, but is not worked
out further. The canon serves to maintain and increase the
tension during the long coda, and it is repeated with a small
rhythmical modification seventeen bars later. More traces of it
can be detected after a further seventeen bars, but it is now
becoming absorbed into the prevailing harmonic style.

*Eight Variations on the Trio 'Tändeln und Scherzen', from the Opera
'Soliman II oder Die Drei Sultaninnen' bv Süssmayer (1799):
Variation VIII*

This variation opens in the style of a fugue and for a little
way continues as one. It is for three voices, and the Subject
follows the Theme quite closely. The first bar is converted into
a syncopation, possibly a development of the opening of Variation VII. The rhythm of 2 reverses that of bar 2 of the Theme,
so that the semiquavers come at the end. The quavers in 3

derive clearly from the Theme and 4 acts as a codetta. The three principal bars of the Subject are thus given different rhythms.

A tonal Answer enters in the alto at 5, but Beethoven cleverly avoids introducing the E flat at 7^1, which would have given too much weight to the key of B flat, and made the return to F for the third entry more difficult. One must assume that the 'mistakes' in the Answer result from a deliberate subordination of it to the needs of the soprano, because 15 and 18 show that Beethoven knew the correct form of the Answer.

Consecutive sixths between the upper parts in 11 ff. foreshadow the nature of this fugato which is not highly contrapuntal. The bass uses the last part of the Subject in sequence through a short Episode leading to a short Middle Section at 16. Here the soprano has the Subject, which appears over a free bass, derived from 4.

In the Episode in 19 ff., the alto echoes the end of the Subject, followed by the soprano (21^2 f.), which elides a bar. This makes the cadential approach to the dominant pedal in 23 ff. more tidy. Over this pedal the upper parts alternate the rhythm of 1 f. in a recognizable melodic shape to 31, where the fugal writing ends.

Sonata in E, Op. 14, No. 1 (1799): 3rd Movement, Bars 14–18^1

This short canon at the octave is directly based on the second part of the main Theme and forms part of the first episode before the first return of the Theme. The two-bar phrase is repeated an octave lower but breaks off as soon as it has effected the cadence of dominant seventh to tonic. The episode, including the canon, is recapitulated in the subdominant in 91 ff., of which the canon occupies 91–95^1.

Sonata in G, Op. 14, No. 2 (1799): 1st Movement, Bars 70–72

The opening figure of this movement is here in the Development section used canonically at the octave for one bar and then repeated. As the B and G sharp are only decorative, the apparent crudities of harmony can be discounted, and the little phrase is revealed as the dominant seventh chord in B flat, which is sustained in this seemingly contrapuntal way (cf. the chord in the Sonata in E flat, Op. 7, discussed on pages 152 f.).

Sonata in B flat, Op. 22 (1800): 4th Movement, Bars 80²–95¹

The movement is a Rondo and this short passage of invertible counterpoint occurs in the second episode. Shedlock repro-duces* the following sketch for this section:

Ex. 119

Beethoven removes the rigidity of this sketch by making the upper part begin a quaver later. The decorated resolution is made more effective by being rewritten in demisemiquavers in the final version. The order of the two halves of the sketch is also reversed. The original sketch is more closely referred to rhythmically in the inversion (84² ff.). The two-part counter-point is continued, with both parts in thirds, based on the lower part in the above sketch, and contrived sequentially. Contrary motion adds to the effectiveness and strength of these bars until the harmony is resumed at 94².

Fifteen Variations with Fugue, Op. 35 (1802)

(a) Variation V, Bars 8²–12²

This short passage of imitative writing is based on the dominant seventh chord (now in arpeggio form) that begins the second half of the Theme, and at first hearing gives the impression of real contrapuntal writing.

(b) Variation VII

This variation is headed *Canone all' ottava*. It looks back to the contrapuntal style of the *Introduzione* (Variations *a due*, *a tre*, and *a quattro*) and forward to the Finale *Alla Fuga*. However, as a canon, it suffers a break for the dominant seventh chords at the beginning of the second half. The resemblance to the Theme is cleverly disguised, though it can be traced on careful inspection:

* 'Beethoven's Sketch Books', *Musical Times*, XXXV, 596 (1st September 1894).

Ex. 120

Variation VII

Theme

The harmonic basis of the first half is simple: tonic and dominant, which is the foundation of the Bass of the Theme. It is seen that the canon acts as a variation of both Theme and Bass.

The little rhythm in 4 is derived from bar 7 of the Theme. The last four bars of the canon follow the outline of the Theme much more closely, though the top E flat in the upper part at 13^2 instead of the expected F a seventh lower provides an effective high-point for the phrase and avoids a too rigid adherence to the Theme. The whole canon is a lively creation, not in the least stuffily academic.

Sonata in F minor, Op. 57 (1804): 3rd Movement

(a) *Bars 96–98¹, 158–163¹*

For a fleeting moment there is a suggestion of counterpoint as the left hand imitates the right an octave below, but both hands fall in sixths immediately. These bars are repeated an octave higher at 100. At 158 the same imitation occurs in F minor, but the two parts maintain comparative independence until 163¹. The original abortive counterpoint is recapitulated in F minor at 288–290¹ and 292–294¹.

(b) *Bars 122²–125²*

The figure which opens the second part at 118 is used in the manner of a canon at the octave at a crotchet's distance between both hands, but it is not developed further.

Thirty-two Variations in C minor (1806)

(a) *Variation XVII*

In this variation Beethoven takes the first four notes of the Theme and adds several notes between the third and fourth notes, so making a phrase of nearly two bars. This phrase, or the rhythm of it, is repeated in each bar of the variation. There is no attempt to extend the complexity of the counterpoint, and the whole is set over an Alberti bass, which appears in the treble at the end.

(b) Variation XXII

This variation is in the form of a canon at the octave, which is maintained throughout. It can easily be followed since each bar contains the same scalewise motif. This must have simplified its composition considerably. The extension of the scale by a crotchet in 6 f. emphasizes the high-point of the Theme and reminds the listener most clearly of the Theme at this point.

Sonata in E flat, Op. 81a (1809): 3rd Movement, Bars 103²–107

This little passage in the Development section of the movement consists of imitations based on bar 11 of this movement. The voices consist therefore of chords in arpeggio form and combine satisfactorily.

Sonata in E minor, Op. 90 (1814): 2nd Movement
(a) Bars 56–59¹, 196–199¹

A little point is introduced in the right hand, imitated an octave below by the left, but both parts immediately continue in tenths and break off only to approach the cadence. The procedure is repeated in another key at 196.

(b) Bars 211²–217¹

Five entries of a figure based on part of the main theme of this movement (bars 2²–4¹) follow each other at one-bar intervals, and each one is different from all the others, a remarkable piece of adaptation.

(c) Bars 221²–228²

Just before the final return of the main theme occurs this small canon at the octave. The rising thirds which it incorporates are derived from the opening of the main theme. Altogether, the two-bar phrase is a decorated form of the dominant seventh chord (first inversion) of E major. This phrase is stated three times in each part before the upper part breaks off to lead back to the first theme.

(d) Bars 283–286[1]

During the coda of the movement appears this short passage of imitation, which uses bars 8[2]–10 for its motif. It occurs in the only part of the movement which is marked *ritardando*. Coming just after a final cadence in the tonic, it sounds like a *stretto* of a fugue. The entry is four-fold, but is not extended into anything more fully developed, once the top note has been reached. There is no attempt at answering a fifth or fourth above; it is quite free. As a result, there is a repeated note at the end of the tenor and alto motifs. This becomes so established that the repeated note is kept in the soprano, which otherwise has the notes of the original entry. A decoration of the chord progression follows, which leads to a more effective resumption of the semiquavers.

Sonata in A, Op. 101 (1816): 2nd Movement, Bars 58–84[1]

This canon appears as the principal part of the Trio section of this movement, and for it Nottebohm has quoted* the following sketch:

Ex. 121

* 'Ein Skizzenbuch aus den Jahren 1815 und 1816', *Zweite Beethoveniana*, pp. 342 f.

The most outstanding difference between this and the final version is the original intention of modulating to D minor at the half-way point, possibly with the hope of avoiding a too sudden return to F major, so recently heard as the key of the march. The G flat in bar 1 of the sketch seems unnecessary and even gloomy; Beethoven later decides to omit it and introduces the canon diatonically. As in the first five bars of the sketch, so in 55–59 there is no start of a continuing canon. Only in 59 does the bass begin imitating the previous treble (58). Yet, as the treble of 58 is part of a beautiful phrase begun in 57, one would hardly expect the imitation to begin half-way through the phrase. But the treble of 59 imitates the bass of 58 also. Doubt arises about which part is actually starting the canon. The listener hearing the work for the first time will not, of course, have realized that there is to be a canon. These five bars should therefore be treated as an aural preparation for the strictness of a canon after the free style of the march. They are transitional and show Beethoven's artistic consideration. Bar 4^{3-4} of the sketch shows a diminution of the alto part in the bass, but the alto is later removed in the interests of clarifying the canonic preparations.

The sketch is substantially the same as the final version until bar 7(= 61). 58 and many other bars provide other instances of the eradication of rigidity in the later form, principally by introducing a dotted rhythm. After the canon has begun in earnest in 60, Beethoven modulates from 61 to F major instead of D minor. In 61 he repeats the B flat in the upper part, and goes on to make such effective use of the D flat falling to C in both parts that the relationship of $61–63^2$ with bars 3^3 f. of the march is unmistakable:

Ex. 122

The manner in which 64 repeats 63 an octave lower seems to reflect the similar repetition of bars 4 f. of the march in bars 6 f. The joining of the two halves of the canon in the sketch seems naïve, and the final version distinctly improves on it. The octave leap between F's remains the only common feature.

The second half of the canon is virtually the same as in the sketch until 69 (= sketch, bar 15). This time the bass leads and the distance between the voices is doubled and the material of 58 f. is fully worked into the canon. This explains why the voices are now at a bar's distance. In 68 the F sharps are dropped in the final version. Though they appeared in the sketch, they were not included in the bass of the previous bar. They would have been inappropriate there, and have caused a false relation with the treble at the end of the bar. Beethoven was therefore writing his canon free as to intervals, but in the final version at 68^{1-2} he decides to maintain the exact shape, even at the expense of momentarily mixing D minor with G minor.

From 70 the distance is narrowed to a half-bar again, according to the intention shown in the sketch. The bass still leads in the final version, however. The one-bar sequential

motif is made more vital and the climax at 73^1 is given strength
by the chromatic rise.

At 76 the first part of the Trio is recapitulated. The inner F
pedal is placed in the treble with a trill, while the moving parts
are placed together in the left hand. They are transposed up an
octave at 78 to prevent a muddy sound. From 79 the bass
precedes the treble and, suitably transposed, the canon ends
at 84^1 in B flat. This section is not to be repeated, as was the
first (55–64), though a beginning is suggested. Instead the
music works back to the march.

Clavierstück in B flat (1818): Bars 30–33

This short piece was written as Beethoven was beginning or
about to begin the Sonata in B flat, Op. 106. Towards the end
are these few bars of two-part counterpoint. At every point
there is a fine rhythmical contrast between the two parts. The
theme is based on bars 5 f., and the bass adds a rhythm derived
from bars 1 and 3. The semiquaver rests add to the spright-
liness of the passage, which soon returns to a harmonic style.

Sonata in B flat, Op. 106 (1818–19)

(a) 1st Movement, Bars 137^4–176^3

Though the sketch-book that Nottebohm consulted is so full
of sketches for this work, he quotes* only one sketch which
relates to this fugato. It is as follows:

Ex. 123

However, he does tell us† that Beethoven was thinking a great
deal in terms of fugue, both in preparation for this and other
compositions, and also in studying text-books and the works of
J. S. Bach. On pages 1, 2, and 7 of the sketch-book are sketches
for the fugue for string quintet, Op. 137, for example:

* 'Skizzen zur Sonate Op. 106', *Zweite Beethoveniana*, p. 126.
† 'Ein Skizzenbuch aus dem Jahre 1817', *Zweite Beethoveniana*, pp. 350 ff.

Ex. 124

On page 4 are two extracts from the fugue in B flat minor from Book I of Bach's *Das Wohltemperirte Clavier*:

Ex. 125

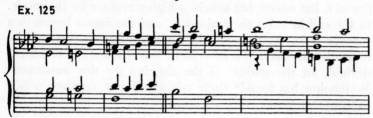

There are two passages from Contrapunctus 4 of Bach's *Die Kunst der Fuge* on page 7:

Ex. 126

The following, which appears on page 8, is taken from Marpurg's text-book *Abhandlung von der Fuge*, Part 2, Tab. XVI, Fig. 1–6:

Ex. 127

Sketches for the first movement of this sonata appear on pages 18–88, followed by sketches for the Ninth Symphony, which contains fugal writing, on pages 92–109.

The sketch for the fugato (Ex. 123) bears little relation to the final version, and indeed gives no indication that there is to be a fugato. Evidently Beethoven leaned towards the dark key of E flat minor, but sought a higher register for the music. In the end he takes the major key, and the fugato begins in a carefree style, even though the register is lower. It should be remembered that in this movement Beethoven is gay and high-spirited. In the middle of the sketches for this movement, Nottebohm has found* these two significant sketches, which confirm this mood:

Ex. 128 (a)

Vi - vat ⸺ ⸺ ru - dol - phus

dieses anfangs durchgeführt u. später 4 stimmiger Chor

Ex. 128 (b)

Vi - vat ru - dol - phus

These are thought by Nottebohm to refer probably to a composition for the Archduke Rudolf's name-day (17th April). The sonata is dedicated to the Archduke, and it can scarcely be gainsaid that these sketches are strikingly similar to the principal theme of this movement, and hence to the fugato which is based on it.

The function of this fugato in the movement is that of a Development section; therefore, as Beethoven chooses the first Subject material on which to comment, it is natural that this motif should be heard repeatedly. The interval of a third is the unifying characteristic of the thematic material of each movement of the sonata. This is seen in 139^{1-2} and in the decorations of 140^2–141^1.

The section begins as a kind of canon, though the interval after the minim is contracted in the lower part. A rising sequence derives from what has been heard, acting as an ex-

---

* 'Skizzen zur Sonate Op. 106', *Zweite Beethoveniana*, pp. 127 f.

tended codetta. Any suggestion that the music is to be a true canon is discarded at 144², when the bass breaks off the imitation. At 146⁴ a soprano part enters in the dominant, attended exactly similarly by an alto part at 147¹. These two parts form an exact replica of, and answer to, the first two parts for six bars. Only the bass is considered necessary to accompany the upper parts. This lightens the texture, and enables similarity between the upper parts and the previously heard lower parts to become apparent. Even the bass is light at first, in order to help the soprano and alto as much as possible (147–149²). Then at 149³, and correspondingly at 151³, the sequence is added to, as the soprano and alto become established. The alto discontinues imitating the previous bass part at 153² and the soprano diverges at 154², as the music moves towards a re-introduction of the theme at 155⁴. Meanwhile the bass adds its accompaniment of filled-in thirds without any rest.

In the next section, it is again the first six bars which receive the strictest treatment. This time, alto and bass appear in parallel motion, two octaves and a third apart, as do, a bar later, soprano and tenor. In this way, they are made to dovetail, another example of the simplified counterpoint of Fux and Albrechtsberger. Beethoven omits a low G to introduce the tenor (156⁴), more to avoid muddiness than a doubled major third. A too great separation of the upper from the lower parts causes him to tie the E flat into 158, rather than rise a sixth, and also the G into 162, where the tie proves a great advantage to the player in leaping to the second crotchet an octave lower in the right hand. In this section the sequence is heard, as it were, in *stretto*.

A kind of episode occurs in the soprano and tenor at 162², joined by the alto and bass when they become available in the next bar. It is based on the familiar rhythm of 140²–141¹ over a rising bass, until a Middle Section in the relative minor at 166⁴. Now, soprano and alto join in thirds answered, as usual, a bar later, by tenor and bass in thirds. At 172³ the soprano minim is changed to F. The expected E natural is impossible after the tenor's move to E flat and the natural tendency of the leading note to rise to the tonic of F minor is emphasized by this chromaticism.

The filled-in thirds finally come into their own, as all four parts give them out for three more bars in double thirds (occasionally sixths) in contrary motion to the end of the fugato (173^2–176^3).

(b) 2nd Movement, Bars 54^3–63^1, 71^3–81^1

Nottebohm quotes* the following sketch for this little passage:

Ex. 129

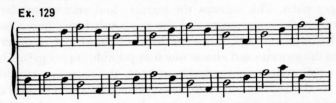

It shows, as he says, that it was conceived like a canon. It seems also to have some slight connexion with a previous sketch† for this movement, in which a fugue in this key (B flat minor) was contemplated:

Ex. 130

auch könnte am Ende
Rondo moderato u. als
Episode Fuge in. B moll

The present little canon appears to be all that is left of that original intention, but at the time Beethoven wrote the above sketch (Ex. 130), he was not intending to write the great fugue for the last movement if one can judge from this sketch:†

Ex. 131

Zwischensatz oder Abschnitt
st. . . . im letzten Stück

---

* 'Skizzen zur Sonate Op. 106', *Zweite Beethoveniana*, pp. 130 f.
† Ibid., p. 129.

The sketches that relate to the fugue of the fourth movement do not appear in the sketch-book until after those of the second and third movements and also those for the introduction to the fourth movement.

The canon under review is, in the final version, just the same as the sketch, apart from some syncopation at the beginning. It is repeated in the relative major at 71^3, and incorporates a return to B flat minor, ending at 80^1. An extra bar in the left hand echoes the end of the canon in the right hand. As a canon it is, of course, quite simple, the theme being merely a chord in arpeggio form.

(c) 4th Movement, Bar 2

This short passage is part of the introduction to the great fugue. The introduction provides a transition from the sublimity of the Adagio (3rd movement) to the forthcoming fugue. Therefore it consists of small outbursts of a few bars each. In this and the next passage, Beethoven is already getting the listener used to contrapuntal styles. These phrases, unbarred in demisemiquavers, are canonical in character. The canon is at the interval, so frequent with Beethoven, of an octave, and at a crotchet's distance. It breaks off after three crotchets, but the strong impression of a canon remains.

(d) 4th Movement, Bars 3-7

This example follows almost immediately on the previous passage and is in the manner of a two-part invention. After three bars, two other voices join in with related material, though not in exact imitation. To do so would have presupposed a more extended working-out of this theme. Beethoven uses these extra voices only as a means of building up the *crescendo*.

Sonata in E, Op. 109 (1820)

(a) 2nd Movement, Bars 70-96

The theme for this short canon is the bass of the first four bars of this movement. It is also heard at 66, immediately before the canon begins. The treatment at 70 is sequential with the result that it forms, in effect, a long descending scale. An upper part answers it a fourth above two bars later, free as to intervals, and the whole is set over a rolling dominant pedal.

During the third statement, at 79, the pedal changes to C giving an interrupted cadence. For the soprano to continue its sequence downwards (80–83) would make the sound muddy, even if not inaudible (the dynamic indication is already *piano*). Moreover, it would be unsatisfactory in terms of C major. With great ingenuity, Beethoven makes a virtue out of necessity. He makes the soprano continue the canon at the octave. This is not too novel, because 74 ff. of the alto are also at the octave from 72 ff. of the soprano.

The third statement in the soprano starts with the A below, instead of above, middle C. Schenker says* that the real thought here is the upper A, though Tovey doubts this.† Schenker adds that the lower A is in the interest of true key-board-writing and is a means of enabling the alto's dotted crotchets in 80 to continue the entry at 78 naturally. These points seem borne out by Beethoven's having written the soprano A (80) in the left-hand stave. The lower A is used originally then as a concession to the player but, according to Schenker,‡ by including this A under the phrase-mark of the second statement, Beethoven makes the two voices in 79 f. seem inverted in 81 f. This halving of the 4-bar motif ends the canon with aural satisfaction.

Then follow various imitations and inversions of the main motif as the music works out related material towards a re-capitulation of the first part of the movement.

(b) 3rd Movement, Variation III

This variation is in invertible counterpoint, and its thirty-two bars follow closely the sixteen bars of the Theme with the repeats written out in full. As Nagel shows,§ the Theme is seen clearly in the variation:

Ex. 132

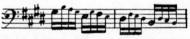

* H. Schenker, *Die letzten fünf Sonaten von Beethoven, Op. 109*, 1913, p. 38.
† D. F. Tovey, *A Companion to Beethoven's Pianoforte Sonatas*, p. 264.
‡ Op. cit., loc. cit.
§ W. Nagel, *Beethoven und seine Klaviersonaten*, 2nd edn. (1924), II, 333.

In order to follow the Theme so closely, various minor adjustments have to be made in the inversions, for example, the lower part in 4 and the upper part in 8.

For the repeat of the first half of the variation (9–16), Beethoven makes a variation on the variation, by amplifying one of the parts. The rhythm of this amplification is retained in the second half (17–32). In this half of the variation, Beethoven varies the technique instead of the material, and so makes the whole of the repeat (25–32) an inversion of 17–24. This procedure is suggested because the two halves of the second half of the Theme do not correspond as closely as those of the first half.

(c) Variation IV

This variation consists of constantly overlapping repetitions of the opening motif, in much the same style as Variation XVII of the Thirty-two Variations in C minor (see pages 157 f.). The counterpoint is not worked out more fully than that, but the whole has a serene effect, enhanced particularly as the hands diverge in 5–7. The polyphonic style predominates in the first half of the variation and occurs only slightly in the second half, which gives the listener a rest before the highly contrapuntal variation which follows.

(d) Variation V

On page 78 of the first of three sketch-books for the years 1819 to 1822, appears a sketch for this variation:*

Ex. 133

The variation was clearly intended to be contrapuntal, though perhaps not as highly so as it finally became. The point in this sketch follows the melodic line of the Theme very closely, but in the final version it becomes more angular by incorporating the C sharp from the alto part of bar 1 of the Theme. The plan of the variation is the same as in the previous four variations,

* G. Nottebohm, 'Drei Skizzenhefte aus den Jahren 1819 bis 1822', *Zweite Beethoveniana*, p. 462.

except that the second half is repeated twice, to make a total of forty bars.

The opening motif in the tenor is repeated *stretto*-wise in every bar for the first six bars, with suitable modifications. Before the bass joins in with the motif, it moves in rising thirds, basically mirroring the tenor, which increases the tension.

At 9 comes the repetition of these bars. To this a new quaver counterpoint is added in the bass after the manner of third species of strict counterpoint and this moves to the soprano in 11. At this point, the motif is repeated an octave higher and, somewhat after the principle in the bass at 6, the second bar becomes detached to form a rising one-bar sequence of its own, similarly supported in the soprano and bass by other sequences. A high-point is reached at 16^4, whereupon the second half begins (17), unhampered by other parts.

The motif is not now introduced *stretto*-wise, but appears every two bars. In each of the four entries the second bar is different. The first entry begins with a falling sixth followed by a semitone, and it is noteworthy how the accompanying parts sympathetically include this feature in their outlines:

Ex. 134

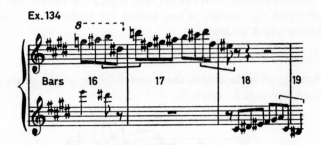

It makes for that unity that underlies a great work. The quaver counterpoint from 9 to 16 is now used extensively.

The essence of 17–24 is repeated in 25–32. A feeling of *stretto* is restored between the upper parts, while the bass provides a quaver counterpoint which again contains a number of large falling intervals, followed by steps (cf. Ex. 134, above). These bars are then repeated, *piano* (33–40).

Sonata in C minor, Op. 111 (1822): 1st Movement

(a) *Bars 35³–48¹*

Nottebohm has shown[*] that the main theme of this movement was originally meant to be the basis of a finale to a three-
movement sonata. He reproduces a sketch from page 76 of the
second of the three sketch-books mentioned on page 169; the
first part of it is quoted here:

Ex. 135

3 tes Stück presto

It seems possible to infer from this that Beethoven was planning
a fugal treatment of the theme.

Pages 3–64 of the third sketch-book are devoted to sketches
for this sonata. No more is mentioned of the material for the
original first two movements and what was to be the third
movement becomes now the first movement. Nottebohm gives[†]
the first of the new sketches as follows:

Ex. 136

This clearly shows a fugal approach. According to Schenker,[‡]
this fugal style was originally intended to be the treatment of

* 'Drei Skizzenhefte aus den Jahren 1819 bis 1822', *Zweite Beethoveniana*, pp. 466–8.

† Ibid., pp. 468 f.

‡ *Die letzten fünf Sonaten von Beethoven, Op. 111*, 1915, p. 36.

the passage under review, as shown on pages 3–5 of the sketch-book.

From pages 7 and 8, Schenker quotes* another sketch to show how Beethoven modifies the keys of the entries from the strict tonic-dominant-tonic:

Ex. 137

This gives Beethoven greater mobility in modulation and does not commit him too severely to the fugal style before the sonata style has had sufficient chance to assert itself. The note-values have been halved (cf. Ex. 136). It only remains now to decorate the quavers with turns and arpeggios to reach the final form, apart from the barring. This is done in the next sketch quoted by Schenker,† which appears on page 11 of the sketch-book:

Ex. 138

This decoration provides a fluent semiquaver counterpoint to the quavers, which are greatly improved in the final version.

* *Die letzten fünf Sonaten von Beethoven, Op. 111*, p. 38. Schenker uses the word *Blatt* and seems to make it here the equivalent of *Seite*.

† Ibid., p. 39.

Beethoven makes a virtue of variation on the original theme out of the necessity of having semiquavers. The whole passage is now less obtrusive than if it had been written in strict fugal style, and it takes its place more comfortably in the movement.

(b) Bars 76–82[1]

This passage occurs at the beginning of the Development section. Schenker quotes* this sketch for the development from page 3 of the sketch-book mentioned above:

Ex. 139

Attempts at *stretto* proved unsuccessful later and the next sketch given* has a different arrangement of the minims, as follows:

Ex. 140

Schenker uses† these illustrations to show the origin of the minims in this passage and to correct the false assumption frequently made that they are an augmentation of the main theme. The opening rise of a third would be too characteristic to be cast aside in three exact repetitions of a minor second, as it is here. That the minims do bear some resemblance to the main theme cannot be denied; Beethoven is relating new material as much as possible to the original motif.

At 76[4] the second note of the main motif is altered from B flat to C. This avoids confusion with the bass at 76[1] and provides a clear change of harmony in the second half of the bar.

Bagatelle in G, Op. 119, No. 6 (1822)

The first two bars afford the only counterpoint in an otherwise harmonic piece. The rising thirds make a very satisfying

* Ibid., p. 44.   † Ibid., loc. cit.

motif and one could have wished that the contrapuntal motif had been extended further.

Thirty-three Variations in C on a Waltz of Diabelli, Op. 120 (1823)

(a) Variation III, Bars 4^2–8^2, 16^2–20^2

Between 4^2 and 8^2 occurs a little canon at the octave over a pedal. The rhythm and contour of the parts are based directly on the opening of the variation. Between 16^2 and 20^2 a series of imitative entries maintains the contrapuntal interest of the variation.

(b) Variation IV

A new motif, derived from the opening of the Waltz, is made the basis of two descending sets of imitative entries from $3/1$ to 7; the second set is necessarily rather more free in order that the general tonality can resemble the corresponding part of the Waltz. At 2^3 a soprano part begins a quaver movement to accompany the lower entries, and once begun, forms a counterpoint to all succeeding entries. In 6^3 f. it allies itself to the motif by running parallel to it.

From 15^3 to 23 the order of entries is reversed and the motif freely inverted, this time to a rolling accompaniment.

(c) Variation VI

This variation begins as a two-part canon at the octave, and the parts are alternately two and three octaves apart. Again the motif is based on the opening of the Waltz. The canon is easily constructed because of the preponderance of arpeggios, but it breaks off at 8^1. The canon is resumed in a free inversion and with reversed order of entry at 16^3. It is broken off again at 24^1.

(d) Variation XI

At first sight this variation appears to begin contrapuntally, but the triplets, derived also from the opening of the Waltz, in fact only decorate the fundamental harmony, though they enter in imitation.

(e) Variation XIX

This variation also opens in the form of a canon at the octave, easily contrived in arpeggios, which continues for eight bars.

Its style and the closeness of the imitation (only a crotchet) recall very strongly Variation VII (*Canone all' ottava*) of the Fifteen Variations with Fugue, Op. 35. The second half begins, as usual, with reversed order of entry and inverted for eight bars, breaks off for a few bars, and hints at the canon again at 29^1.

(*f*) *Variation XX*

Another canon, at the fifteenth and at two bars' distance, opens this variation, and continues until 8^2. A free inner part completes this deep-set harmony. The intervals are not always preserved strictly; at 2^1 Beethoven writes A, which becomes A flat in the top part at 4^1. The A natural keeps the tonality in C major; the A flat does not change it to C minor, but rather enhances the gloominess of the harmony by making a diminished seventh chord.

At 16^2 imitative entries replace a resumption of the canon. The notes used at first correspond to bars $4^3/5^1$ of the Waltz. Beethoven does not continue the counterpoint, in order not to detract from the essential harmonic nature of the variation.

(*g*) *Variation XXIV*

This is the most extensive variation in the set, contrapuntally, apart from Variation XXXII, and is labelled Fughetta. In construction, however, it still follows the usual outward form of division into two equal parts, with repeat signs for each half.

The Subject, made up of six crotchets, opens with the drop of a fourth, which opens the Waltz. Its lack of rhythmic contrast sets the mood of calm for the whole variation. The Answer enters at 3^2, correctly modified, over a Countersubject of quavers. During the entry of the Subject in the bass (5^2–7^1), the alto in 6 fills in two falling thirds and provides the first of many allusions to the Subject, with which the variation abounds. The feeling of *stretto* and mounting interest is constantly present. Beethoven fits in another reference in the bass at 8^1 with a false Answer, while the tenor is making the fourth entry. Above, in the soprano, the two semiquavers amongst all the quavers make a delightfully fresh touch.

After the four entries of the Exposition, there is more than

sufficient time to make a comfortable modulation to the dominant. The music moves to D minor, in which key another false
Answer occurs (11², alto). Carefully but easily sliding out of
this key, Beethoven moves to G major with a third false Answer
in the tenor at 14². He keeps this key ingeniously until the end
of the first half. The interest is maintained by two drops of
a fifth in the soprano, again suggestive of the Answer, at 15²
and 16¹, while the bass contributes a cadential, but similarly
relevant, drop of a fifth. Beethoven thus uses even the most
modest means of making his point clear.

The second half begins with the alto stating the theme inverted (17² ff.). The tenor enters next, only one bar later, with a
variant of the theme. Beethoven is more concerned to make
interesting music here than to be obliged to keep the theme
exactly, as a lesser composer might have been expected to do.
At 20² the soprano gives the true Answer to the inverted
Subject, except that it cannot begin tonally, on G, because the
music is now in D minor. A fourth entry due from the bass is
not given, though the alto makes partial amends at 22¹⁻².
This keeps the listener aware of the theme until a kind of Middle
Section in E minor is made by the tenor at 23². Beethoven
cleverly continues this entry by handing it from voice to voice
in the lower parts:

Ex. 141

Alto

Tenor

Bars 23 24 25

Bass

Incomplete entries follow quickly in the bass (24² f.), tenor
(25² f.), and bass (26² f.), though the last is continued in full
but rhythmically altered:

176

Ex. 142

Bars   26   27   28

This leads immediately into another entry in the bass which includes a variation of the original from 29^2. Another reference to the theme can be seen in the soprano (29 ff.):

Ex. 143

From 30^2 the theme reappears *recto*, incomplete at first as if tentative, in the tenor, and more fully in the soprano, where it can be heard best, in 31^2 f., to end the variation.

(h) Variation XXX

A series of descending entries every half-bar opens this variation in contrapuntal style. As each entry is to begin on E flat, the third entry has to begin on the same E flat as the previous one, to prevent the texture from becoming too widespread and unpianistic, which would result if every new entry began an octave higher. By an ingenious compromise, Beethoven makes the second half of the third entry take its higher octave. In addition, he accompanies the theme a third above for the first three notes to obtain a higher pitch for each succeeding entry, and then a third below for the next two notes, to give the remainder of the theme prominence and to avoid being too close to the fourth entry. This entry is incomplete because the music modulates into D flat. The bass immediately gives an entry in this key at 2^4, closely followed by the soprano at 3^2, after which the contrapuntal interest ends in 4.

At 8^4 begins a series of imitative entries using the same rhythm as before, but in a different melodic shape. Three entries are made to suffice at first. With the *stretto* from the bass at 9^4 the theme undergoes modifications, becoming less distinguishable as the music merges into harmony again.

Bagatelle in B minor, Op. 126, No. 4 (1823–4), Bars 26⁴–33³

In discussing the first sketch, Nottebohm shows★ that the second section, which now numbers 43 bars, originally contained only twenty-four bars, being the first twelve bars and the last twelve bars of the section, as it stands now. In the nineteen missing bars occur a few bars, in which the theme is given a contrapuntal treatment. In this, Beethoven prefers to keep his characteristic opening leap of a fourth, rather than make the adjustment for a tonal Answer. The voices stop sometimes as soon as they have given the two-bar theme, and in any case after the third bar, so that there are never more than three parts sounding together, in spite of five entries. Though the material is reminiscent of Variation V of the finale of the Sonata in E, Op. 109 in its vigour, it is not worked out in a similarly interesting way.   To have done so would have upset the balance of this Bagatelle. The passage is recapitulated exactly at 131⁴.

★ 'Die Bagatellen Op. 126', *Zweite Beethoveniana*, p. 202.

X

CONCLUSION

MUSICAL fashions changed fundamentally between the times of Bach and Beethoven, and even Bach, as is well known, was considered out-of-date in his own time, so that his style was rather the culmination of what was current practice in the seventeenth century.

As a result, Beethoven's early years were spent in a musical atmosphere that had, for most of the eighteenth century, reacted from the baroque style of Bach, and followed new paths. At Bonn, the music of the Mannheim school had a great popularity, as Riemann testifies,* and this influence is traceable even in Beethoven's later works. The music written by the composers of this school was of a completely different style from that of Bach, and especially in the instrumental music contrapuntal and fugal writing was much less prominent.

When Beethoven went to Vienna, he clearly came under the powerful influence of the composers of the Viennese Classical school, chiefly Haydn and Mozart, whose music was also cultivated in Bonn. The Viennese composers, according to Friedrich Deutsch,† while for the most part no longer writing independent fugues, as Bach did, did not abandon the fugal

* H. Riemann, 'Beethoven und die Mannheimer', *Die Musik*, VII, iii. 3 ff., 85 ff. (April 1908).

† F. Deutsch, 'Die Fugenarbeit in den Werken Beethovens', *Studien zur Musikwissenschaft* (Beihefte der Denkmäler der Tonkunst in Österreich), XIV (Beethoven-Zentenarfeier, Vienna (26th–31st March 1927), Festschrift), 97. The author is now known as Frederick D. Dorian.

style completely. With them, fugue in their instrumental works, wherever it appears, is often used for one movement in a cyclic composition, or in the shorter form of a fugato built into the movement. Quite frequently, however, one can find the general homophony relieved by a set of imitative entries for a few bars. As has been seen, such sets of entries are a feature of Beethoven's piano music. In the later music of Hadyn and Mozart in cyclic form there is a growing inclination to use fugue and fugato, and a successful attempt at making the fugal style sound satisfying in this context. There was now taking place a great revival of interest in the potentialities of fugue as a vital element in composition, which has continued to the present day with varying effectiveness in its practical application, and in this sphere Beethoven was to make his individual and powerful contribution.

In designing fugue themes, the Viennese composers tended to repeat short motifs, which gave their subjects a distinct shape, whereas the baroque composers rarely admitted anything having a stiff formality. This could lead to quite simple subjects, completely foreign to the Bach style, and those for the early fugue in C and the Finale *Alla Fuga* of the Fifteen Variations with Fugue, Op. 35, are in this tradition.

The new sonata style of composition encouraged the Viennese Classical composers to write extended modulatory sections in the Development section of a movement in so-called sonata form. This is reflected in their fugues by longer modulating episodes before the arrival of a middle section, as compared with the baroque composers, who would sometimes amplify the importance of the tonic tonality by having a counter-exposition. These longer episodes are to be found also in Beethoven's fugues, as follow : Op. 35, bars 16^1–27 and 47^1–89; Op. 101, bars 160^2–172^2 and 182^1–208^2; Op. 106, bars 71^2–93, 116^3–152, 174^3–207, 223–249, and 306–333; Op. 110, bars 66^2–87^1; and Op. 120, bars 68–85^3.

Deutsch points out[*] that, in the matter of *stretto*, there is no Viennese counterpart to the C major fugue in Book I of Bach's *Das Wohltemperirte Clavier*. It is noteworthy in Beethoven's pianoforte fugues that only one exploits *stretto* to any considerable degree, namely, the finale of the Sonata in B flat, Op. 106.

[*] Op. cit., p. 99.

CONCLUSION

Stretto occurs in the finale of the Sonata in A flat, Op. 110, bars 91² ff. and 101² ff., but the later entries in each case are not full statements of the Subject.

It has been shown* in the preliminary discussion on the fugue in Op. 110 that in design it is a complete novelty. The greatly extended Exposition on the one hand matches approximately the combined length of the Middle and Final Sections on the other, with the return of the *Arioso* occurring in between. The freer style of the Final Section (174² ff.) provides Beethoven with an ideal opportunity of reconciling the intellectual manner of the fugue with the dramatic style of the sonata. In this fugue Beethoven shows a particularly masterly control in the use of technical devices. It begins as a vocal fugue in a restrained style, but after the Exposition it is necessary to prepare the theme for the flourishing keyboard manner of the Final Section. Accordingly, during the Middle Section, Beethoven works out a scheme of diminutions and augmentation. Firstly, at 152, a diminution is heard against an augmentation contrived in such a way that the relationship is at the rate of six diminutions to one augmentation. Secondly, at 168, the effect is that both diminution and augmentation are diminished to notes of half length. This both causes the augmentation to return to the original note-lengths of the Subject and also preserves the ratio of six to one. Finally, at 174², the six-to-one relationship emerges triumphant in the six semiquavers to one dotted crotchet in the Final Section. In other fugues, where the Subject is already of a pianistic nature, this kind of problem does not arise, and Beethoven does not parade technical devices merely for the sake of effect.

If the absorption of the style of the Viennese Classical school was a subconscious part of Beethoven's development as a composer, as exemplified in the fugues under review, there were other considerations of a more personal nature that affected him in relation to fugue in particular.

From the turn of the century, the emphasis of Beethoven's life and work was changed. Faced with incurable and increasing deafness and the appalling knowledge that finally, external musical sounds would not reach him, his whole approach to music deepened. The virtuoso world receded, giving place to

* pp. 95 ff.

that of the composer. As Beethoven's deafness became more and more severe, the dramatic and personal intensity of his compositions grew, reflecting his desperate yet unflinching struggle. Added to this affliction, there were his unhappy love-affairs and, from 1812, violent family disagreements, followed by the guardianship of his nephew, on whose account Beethoven became so deeply involved.

All these in total must have combined to slow down Beethoven's rate of composition after 1812 so that comparatively few major works were written between then and the early part of 1818. During these years one may be sure that Beethoven had reached a stage when he could no longer express himself adequately in the kind of music he had been writing, revolutionary in style as even that was at the time. The search was for still more depth in the content of his music, and he achieved this principally by discovering for himself the possibilities of fugue.

One can only conjecture whether the abstracts on thorough-bass, counterpoint, and fugue which Beethoven made in 1809 were the first stage in this new change in his style towards polyphony. These abstracts, mentioned earlier,* are taken from standard technical treatises of the eighteenth century and form a manual of instruction which was almost certainly used when Beethoven taught the Archduke Rudolf. This return to a specifically contrapuntal line of thought after a space of fourteen years, during eleven of which deafness was closing in, may indeed have suggested to Beethoven a possible solution of the problems of musical self-expression forced upon him by his malady.

A. E. Hull postulates† that, between 1815 and 1818, Beethoven was steeping himself in the works of Bach, and it is true that two passages transcribed from Bach's *Das Wohltemperirte Clavier*, I, 22 (fugue), two passages from *Die Kunst der Fuge* (Contrapunctus 4), and one from Marpurg's *Abhandlung von der Fuge*, showing a theme in contrary and retrograde motion, appear in the same sketch-book as the sketches for the first movement of the Sonata in B flat, Op. 106.‡ Also, Bach's music

* Chapter II, pp. 13 f.
† 'Beethoven's Third Style', *Musical Opinion*, Vol. 47 (1923), pp. 276 ff.
‡ G. Nottebohm, 'Ein Skizzenbuch aus dem Jahre 1817', *Zweite Beethoveniana*, pp. 350 ff.

was rather better known at this time than is generally supposed, according to E. F. Schmid.* He points out that Breitkopf & Härtel issued two volumes of Motets in 1802 and 1803 and that the Baron von Swieten, with whom Beethoven associated in his first years in Vienna, owned the six English and French Suites, and probably the Italian Concerto and the Violin Sonata in A minor, all of which Beethoven presumably came to know. In 1809, Beethoven requested of Breitkopf & Härtel any available scores of the masters, including J. S. Bach. Additional Bach scores were available to Beethoven in the library of the Archduke Rudolf and from Raphael Georg Kiesewetter, a musical friend of Beethoven and a writer on musical history. Beethoven's publishers, Traeg & Hoffmeister, brought out editions of Bach which Beethoven no doubt saw. Nottebohm shows too† that Beethoven was familiar with the Chromatic Fantasy and Fugue, and in a letter to Breitkopf & Härtel, dated 15th October 1810, Beethoven quotes from the Mass in B minor.‡

This indebtedness to Bach, which dates back ultimately to the introduction of *Das Wohltemperirte Clavier* by Neefe, is most clearly seen in the finale of the Sonata in B flat, Op. 106. In this fugue, Beethoven comes most nearly to that Bach-like linear independence of parts which is so largely foreign to the music of the Viennese composers.

Beethoven found in his later works that frequently only by means of fugue could he adequately resolve the conflicts and tensions presented in the earlier movements or variations. Tovey likens§ a fugue in a sonata to a trial scene in a drama, and this often occurs as a climatic point towards the end: it is noticeable that the fugues always come in Beethoven's piano music at or near the end of the compositions. Such trial scenes are the inevitable sequel to the interweavings of the plot, and it is Beethoven's great achievement when he uses fugues, that they also seem the only suitable means of settling the musical issues. This is particularly so in the Sonata in A, Op. 101, in

* 'Beethoven's Bachkenntnis', *Neues Beethoven-Jahrbuch*, V (1933), 64 ff.

† 'Ein Skizzenheft aus dem Jahre 1810', *Zweite Beethoveniana*, p. 286.

‡ *Beethoven's Letters*, ed. by A. C. Kalischer, trans. by J. S. Shedlock, 1909, I, 207.

§ *A Companion to Beethoven's Pianoforte Sonatas*, p. 248.

which the contrapuntal exposition invites a fugal development. A fugue here is so natural that the listener is not made forcibly aware of its introduction. In the two sets of variations, Opp. 35 and 120, the fugues have been prepared at several points by variations which are contrapuntal to a greater or less degree.

In such ways as this, Beethoven succeeded in making his fugues sound perfectly logical in the longer works in which they are set, instead of appearing foreign, as could so easily have happened. Few things could make the fugues seem more at variance with his sonata style than a slavish imitation of Bach, and to judge Beethoven's fugues by the Bach yardstick is utterly unrealistic and irrelevant; the two styles are fundamentally dissimilar. We may be sure that Beethoven studied closely all those works of Bach which were available to him, but he remained true to his own genius by adapting fugal techniques to his special needs, and investing them with all the poetry of which he was capable. The fugues in Beethoven's piano music, particularly the late ones, are then the rich result of the fertilization of the best elements of the Viennese school with those of Bach. They are irreplaceable in those works of Beethoven which rank among his greatest, and always show him to be completely the master in every degree of technique and emotion.

APPENDIXES

APPENDIX A

FINALE *ALLA FUGA*, FIFTEEN VARIATIONS WITH FUGUE, OP. 35
TRANSCRIBED INTO OPEN SCORE

ABBREVIATIONS

Ex.	= Exposition
S.	= Subject (extent shown in first instance by ⌐———¬)
A.	= Answer
C.S.	= Countersubject
R.E.	= Redundant Entry
Ep.	= Episode
M.S.	= Middle Section
F.S.	= Final Section
Th.	= Fugue Theme when not representing S. or A.
aug.	= augmented
dim.	= diminished
abb.	= abbreviated
inv.	= inverted
ext.	= extended
var.	= varied
a, b, etc.	= motifs *a, b,* etc.

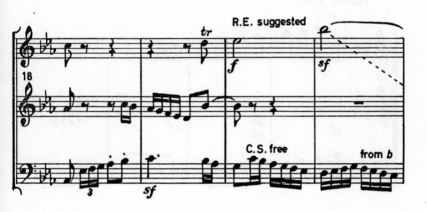

Ep. in sequence

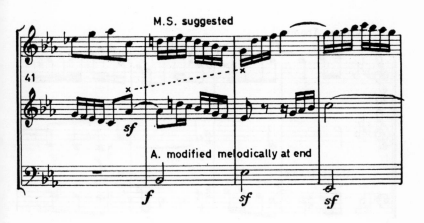

M.S. suggested

A. modified melodically at end

Ep. in sequence

189

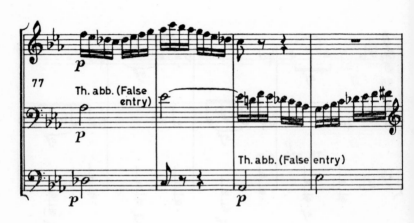

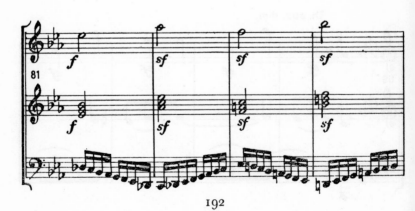

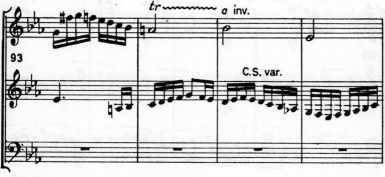

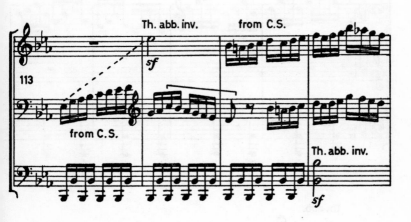

cf. bars 123 – end with
the Tema (2nd section)
and Var. VII (2nd section)
of this work

APPENDIX B

Beethoven's Attitude to Counterpoint and Fugue, as expressed in his own words

The following extracts together with the notes in parentheses are taken mostly from *Beethoven: The Man and the Artist, as revealed in his own words* (compiled and annotated by Friedrich Kerst), 1926, to which the page numbers refer. My own comments, where necessary, appear separately after the extracts concerned.

1. No devil can compel me to write cadences of such a kind. (From notes written in his years of study. Beethoven called the composition of fugues 'the art of making musical skeletons'.) (p. 25.)

2. In order to become a capable composer one must have already learned harmony and counterpoint at the age of from 7 to 11 years, so that when the fancy and emotions awake one shall know what to do according to the rules. (Reported by Schindler as having been put into the mouth of Beethoven by a newspaper of Vienna. Schindler says: 'When Beethoven came to Vienna he knew no counterpoint and little harmony'.) (p. 27.)

In view of its dubious origin, this quotation should be treated as aprocryphal. If it is a true statement of Beethoven's, then it may express his firm opinion on how he would have wished to spend his early years, if he could have lived them again. Originally, of course, it was not expected that Beethoven would become primarily a composer, but a virtuoso pianist; otherwise, his musical training would have taken a more theoretical turn much sooner. It is unlikely that Neefe used Bach's *Das Wohltemperirte Clavier* in any instruction in counterpoint or fugue, but Beethoven's sound knowledge of it as a performer, together with his proficiency at improvization, may have been sufficient to enable him to extemporize a double fugue for Mozart in 1787, and we have only the unreliable Seyfried's word for it that he did so.

3. So far as mistakes are concerned it was never necessary for me to learn Thoroughbass, my feelings were so sensitive from childhood

that I practised counterpoint without knowing that it must be so or could be otherwise. (Note on a sheet containing directions for the use of fourths in suspensions—probably intended for the instruction of Archduke Rudolf.) (p. 27.)

This statement does not accord with the facts of Beethoven's own life, and is impossible to explain without recourse to psychology. It could be that Beethoven was suddenly overcome by an inferiority complex in relation to his friend, patron, and only pupil, but this is scarcely likely. He may have felt, as he reflected on his early years, how obvious and natural are the movements and progressions in music (from which the 'rules' of thoroughbass and counterpoint are deduced), once they become familiar, that he ought not to have needed any instruction. This could then have led to the exaggeration and idealization of his musical childhood.

4. On the whole the carrying out of several voices in strict relationship mutually hinders their progress. (Autumn 1812 in Diary of 1812–1818.) (pp. 29 f.)

This probably refers to fugal writing, though the quotation is too short for any further explanation.

5. Kerst reports Czerny as saying of Beethoven: 'His reading of the scores of Händel and Gluck and the fugues of Bach was unique, inasmuch as he put a polyphony and spirit into the former which gave the works a new form.' (p. 36.)

6. That you are going to publish Sebastian Bach's works is something which does good to my heart, which beats in love of the great and lofty art of this ancestral father of harmony; I want to see them soon. (January, 1801, to Hofmeister, in Leipzic.) (p. 55.)

This seems to suggest that Beethoven believed and recognized that Bach conceived his music on a harmonic, rather than contrapuntal, basis, though it may be objected that 'harmony' is used here in the general sense of a satisfying co-ordination of sounds.

7. To *make* a fugue requires no particular skill (to Holz); in my study days I made dozens of them. But the fancy wishes also to assert its privileges, and to-day a new and really poetical element must be introduced into the traditional form. (A. W. Thayer: *The Life of Ludwig van Beethoven*, II, 365.)

This observation, made to Holz, is one of the most illuminating on Beethoven's attitude to fugue and is the clue to a fuller understanding of the fugues in all his later works. It shows that his approach to fugue was not at all academic; he did not aim to write *fugues d'école*. His fugues are solely the means of expressing some of his most lofty ideas and not moulds into which he could pour them. Beethoven mastered fugue without its mastering him.

APPENDIX C

The State of the Sketch-books

It is sometimes fatally easy to try to date the sketches for a work merely from their position in a sketch-book, or to conclude that sketches that appear to follow each other were, in fact, composed in that order.

Albert Levinsohn suggests,* from his study of certain sketches, that Beethoven very rarely, if at all, took a new, bound, empty book and wrote in an orderly manner on successive pages. Instead he would take the nearest loose sheets available and, in due course, bind them together, not necessarily in the right order. The many empty spaces left on these sheets would be used later, as occasion required. Beethoven may have returned to a sketch-book years after it was bound.

Paul Mies observes† how Beethoven would start a new work on a new page. This would mean that he would complete one page with sketches for a certain work, miss the next page if already devoted to another work, and resume the first work on a third page. We know from Beethoven's own words‡ that he usually had three or four works 'on the stocks' at once.

Nottebohm gives§ three reasons for the study of the sketch-books: (1) the determination of the date of composition, (2) the disclosure of works started but not finished, and (3) their value as a glimpse into Beethoven's workshop. Levinsohn shows‖ how Nottebohm himself fell into the trap of assuming that sketches were necessarily composed in the order in which they appear. In one sketch-book

* 'Die Entstehungszeit der Ouverture zu Leonore Nr. 1 Op. 138, mit anschliessenden kritischen Bemerkungen zu Nottebohm's Beethoveniana', *Vierteljahrsschrift für Musikwissenschaft*, IX (1893), 165.

† *Beethoven's Sketches: an Analysis of his Style, based on a study of his sketch-books*, trans. by D. L. Mackinnon, London, 1929, pp. 147 f.

‡ *Beethoven: The Man and the Artist, as revealed in his own words*, compiled and annotated by F. Kerst, 1926, p. 28.

§ *Zweite Beethoveniana*, 1887, Einleitung, p. IX.

‖ Op. cit., pp. 164 f.

which Nottebohm describes,[*] he links together in time sketches for *Wellingtons Sieg* (or *Die Schlacht bei Vittoria*), written in 1813 and published in 1816, which appear on one side of a page, with those for the Sonata in A flat, Op. 110 and the Mass in D, both of which were not sketched until after 1816 and which appear on the other side.

Further evidence that Beethoven worked on a number of compositions at once may be adduced from an article by K. Huschke,[†] in which he states that at Beethoven's death, he had sketched, planned, or discussed the following works: Tenth Symphony (wholly instrumental), Eleventh Symphony (probably with a chorus in the last two movements), music to Faust, an oratorio on *The Triumph of the Cross* (*Der Sieg des Kreuzes*) and probably other oratorios, a Mass and a Requiem, an opera *Melusine* (with libretto by Grillparzer) and possibly others on *Macbeth* and *Lear,* and an overture on the name *BACH*. Little pianoforte music had been planned, except for a sonata for four hands which had been sketched. One movement of a quintet had been completed, and Beethoven might have taken up the sketches for a Violoncello Sonata (*Pastorale*), which he made in 1815.

A minor point about the sketches is that Beethoven rarely prefixed a clef or key-signature before a sketch, but it is usually obvious, even in a single-stave sketch, which clef is meant and what key-signature is understood, especially if there are accidentals. However, Beethoven often omitted necessary accidentals, and this, together with a certain amount of illegibility resulting from the speed at which he must often have tried to capture his teeming inspiration, inevitably leads to doubt about his intentions in some cases.

[*] Ibid., loc. cit.; Levinsohn refers to G. Nottebohm, *Zweite Beethoveniana*, p. 463.

[†] 'Was uns durch Beethovens vorzeitigen Tod verlorenging', *Die Musik*, XIX, ii. 470 ff. (January 1920).

BIBLIOGRAPHY

ALBRECHTSBERGER, J. G.

Gründliche Anweisung zur Composition, Breitkopf, Leipzig, 1790.
Collected Writings on Thorough-bass, Harmony and Composition, for Self-instruction, edited by I. Ritter von Seyfried, a translation by S. Novello with the musical portion revised by V. Novello, 3 vols. bound in one, Novello, Ewer & Co., London, 1855.

BACH, C. P. E.

Versuch über die wahre Art das Clavier zu spielen, 2 parts: Part I, C. F. Henning, Berlin, 1753; Part II, G. L. Winter, Berlin, 1762. Second edition, 2 parts, E. B. Schwickert, Leipzig, 1787, 1797.
Essay on the True Art of playing Keyboard Instruments, a translation and edition of the above by W. J. Mitchell, Cassell, London, 1949. Second edition, Cassell, London, 1951.

BEETHOVEN, L. VAN

Beethovens sämmtliche Briefe, a critical edition with explanatory notes by Dr. A. C. Kalischer, 5 vols., Schuster & Löffler, Berlin, 1906–11.
Beethoven's Letters, a translation of the 1st edition of the above by J. S. Shedlock, 2 vols., Dent, London, 1909.
Ludwig van Beethovens sämmtliche Briefe, edited by E. Kastner, Hesse & Becker, Leipzig, 1910. Second edition revised and enlarged by Dr. J. Kapp, Hesse & Becker, Leipzig, 1923.
Beethoven im eigenen Wort, compiled by F. Kerst, Schuster & Löffler, Berlin and Leipzig, 1904. Second enlarged edition, Schuster & Löffler, Berlin, 1905.
Beethoven: The Man and the Artist, as revealed in his own words, compiled by F. Kerst, a translation of the above by H. E. Krehbiel, Gay & Bird, London (printed by B. W. Huebsch, New York), 1906. Second impression with a different title-page, Godfrey Bles, London (printed in U.S.A.), 1926.
Beethoven's Own Words, compiled and annotated by P. Kruseman, translated by H. Antcliffe, Hinrichsen, London (printed in Holland), 1947.
Beethoven: Fugue in C (hitherto unpublished), edited and arranged from the original autograph manuscript by Jack Werner, Joseph Williams, London, 1956. See also under DICKINSON, A. E. F.

Ludwig van Beethoven: Klaviersonaten, after the manuscripts and the original printings reconstrued by H. Schenker, 4 vols., Universal-Edition, Vienna, 1934. New edition revised by E. Ratz, 4 vols., Universal-Edition, Vienna, 1945. See also under SCHENKER, H.

Beethoven: Sonatas for Pianoforte, edited by H. Craxton and D. F. Tovey, 3 vols., Associated Board of the Royal Schools of Music, London, 1931.

Analytische Darstellung der Fuge aus Beethoven's Sonate, Op. 106, 3rd Appendix in the Supplement to *Das Wohltemperierte Klavier,* Book I, arranged and explained by F. Busoni (Band I of *Johann Sebastian Bach: Klavierwerke,* new edition by F. Busoni and others), Breitkopf & Härtel, Leipzig-Wiesbaden, 1897.

Beethoven: Variationen für Klavier zu 2 Händen, edited by Adolf Ruthardt, 2 vols., C. F. Peters, Leipzig, n.d.

Ludwig van Beethoven's Werke, complete, critically revised throughout and authorized edition (usually referred to as the *Gesamtausgabe*), 25 vols., Breitkopf & Härtel, Leipzig, various dates.

BEHREND, W.
Ludwig van Beethoven's Pianoforte Sonatas, translated by I. Lund, Dent, London, 1927.

BEKKER, P.
Beethoven, Schuster & Löffler, Berlin and Leipzig, 1911 (now published by Deutsche Verlags-Anstalt, Stuttgart).
Beethoven, a translation and adaptation of the above by M. M. Bozman, Dent, London, 1925.

BLOM, E.
Beethoven's Pianoforte Sonatas Discussed, Dent, London, 1938.

DANNREUTHER, E.
'Notes on the Text of Beethoven', article in the *Monthly Musical Record,* London, Vol. II, 1872.

DAVID, H. T., and MENDEL, A., editors
The Bach Reader: A Life of Johann Sebastian Bach in Letters and Documents, W. W. Norton & Co. Inc., New York, 1945.

DEUTSCH, F. (DORIAN, F. D.)
'Die Fugenarbeit in den Werken Beethovens', article in *Studien zur Musikwissenschaft,* the supplement issued by the Gesellschaft zur Herausgabe von Denkmälern der Tonkunst in Österreich, Vienna, Vol. XIV, 1927, published in connexion with the Beethoven centenary, Vienna, 26th–31st March 1927.

DICKINSON, A. E. F.
'Beethoven's Early Fugal Style', article in the *Musical Times,* London, Vol. 96, 1955. This article contains a transcription of Beethoven's Fugue in C.

Bach's Fugal Works: with an Account of Fugue before and after Bach, Pitman, London, 1956.

ERNST, G.

'Beethovens Instrumentalfugen', No. II of 'Beethoven-Studien', articles in *Die Musik*, Berlin, Vol. X, iii. 1911.

FRIEDLAND, M.

Zeitstil und Persönlichkeitsstil in den Variationwerken der Musikalischen Romantik—Zur Geistesgeschichte und Schaffenspsychologie der Romantik, Inaugural dissertation, Sammlung musikwissenschaftlicher Einzeldarstellungen, Heft 14, Leipzig, 1930.

FRIMMEL, T., editor

Beethoven-Handbuch, 2 vols., Breitkopf & Härtel, Leipzig, 1926.

FUX, J. J.

Gradus ad Parnassum, J. P. van Ghelen, Vienna, 1725.

Steps to Parnassus, a translation and edition of the first part (The Study of Counterpoint) of the above by A. Mann, W. W. Norton & Co. Inc., New York, 1943, and Dent, London (printed in U.S.A.), 1944.

The Study of the Fugue: A Dialogue, a translation and edition of the second part (The Study of the Fugue) by A. Mann, four articles in the *Musical Quarterly*, New York, Vols. XXXVI and XXXVII, 1950–1.

HESS, W.

'Welche Werke Beethovens fehlen in der Breitkopf und Härtelschen Gesamtausgabe?', article in *Neues Beethoven-Jahrbuch*, Brunswick, Vol. VII, 1937, Vol. IX, 1939.

'Check-List of Beethoven's Compositions not contained in the Gesamtausgabe', article in *Hinrichsen's Music Book*, Vol. VIII, Hinrichsen, London, 1954.

HULL, A. E.

'Beethoven's Third Style', article in *Musical Opinion*, London, Vol. 47, 1923.

HUSCHKE, K.

'Was uns durch Beethovens vorzeitigen Tod verlorenging', article in *Die Musik*, Berlin, Vol. XIX, ii. 1920.

JEPPESON, K.

Counterpoint, translated by G. Haydon, Prentis Hall, Inc., New York, 1939, and Williams & Norgate, London, 1950.

KASTNER, E.

Bibliotheca Beethoveniana: Versuch einer Beethoven-Bibliographie, Breitkopf & Härtel, Leipzig, 1913. Second edition revised (with a supplement) by T. Frimmel, Breitkopf & Härtel, Leipzig, 1925.

KINSKY, G.

Das Werk Beethovens, thematic and bibliographical catalogue of his collected complete compositions: after the death of the author completed and edited by Hans Halm, G. Henle Verlag, Munich-Duisburg, 1955.

KIRNBERGER, J. P.
Die Kunst des reinen Satzes in der Musik, 2 parts, C. F. Voss, Berlin, 1771–9, and Chemische Druckerei, Vienna, 1793.

LEVINSOHN, A.
'Die Entstehungszeit der Ouverture zu Leonore Nr. 1 Op. 138, mit anschliessenden kritischen Bemerkungen zu Nottebohm's Beethoveniana', article in *Vierteljahrsschrift für Musikwissenschaft*, Leipzig, Vol. IX, 1893.

MACARDLE, D. W.
Beethoven Abstracts (typescript deposited at the British Museum, the Library of Congress, and the New York Public Library), British Museum press-mark: W.P. 15583.

MARPURG, F. W.
Abhandlung von der Fuge, 2 parts, A. Haude and J. C. Spener, Berlin, 1753, 1754.
Handbuch bey dem Generalbasse und der Composition, 3 parts, Schützen's Wittwe und Lange, Berlin, 1755–8.
Anhang zum Handbuche bey dem Generalbasse und der Composition, Lange, Berlin, 1760.

MIES, P.
Die Bedeutung der Skizzen Beethovens zur Erkenntnis seines Stiles, Breitkopf & Härtel, Leipzig, 1925.
Beethoven's Sketches: An Analysis of his Style, based on a Study of his Sketch-books, a translation of the above by D. L. Mackinnon, Oxford University Press, London, 1929.
'Die Bedeutung von Skizzen, Briefen, und Erinnerungen für die stilkundliche Forschung', article in *Neues Beethoven-Jahrbuch*, Brunswick, Vol. VIII, 1938.

MISCH, L.
'Fugue and Fugato in Beethoven's Variation Form', article in the *Musical Quarterly*, New York, Vol. XLII, 1956.

MÜLLER-BLATTAU, J.
'Beethoven und die Variation', article in *Neues Beethoven-Jahrbuch*, Brunswick, Vol. V, 1933.

NAGEL, W.
Beethoven und seine Klaviersonaten, 2 vols., H. Beyer & Söhne, Langensalza, 1903, 1905. Second edition, H. Beyer & Söhne, Langensalza, 1923, 1924.

NEWMAN, E.
The Unconscious Beethoven, Parsons, London, 1927.

NOTTEBOHM, M. G.

Ein Skizzenbuch von Beethoven, Breitkopf & Härtel, Leipzig, 1865.

Ein Skizzenbuch Beethovens aus dem Jahre 1803, Breitkopf & Härtel, Leipzig, 1880.

Zwei Skizzenbücher von Beethoven aus den Jahren 1801 bis 1803, a 2nd impression of the two preceding volumes combined as a new edition, with a foreword by P. Mies, Breitkopf & Härtel, Leipzig, 1924.

Thematisches Verzeichnis der im Druck erschienenen Werke L. v. Beethovens, Breitkopf & Härtel, Leipzig, 1850. Second edition, enlarged with chronological and bibliographical notes, Breitkopf & Härtel, Leipzig, 1868. Second edition (2nd impression), bound with *Bibliotheca Beethoveniana*, by E. Kastner, Breitkopf & Härtel, Leipzig, 1913. Second edition (3rd impression), bound with *Bibliotheca Beethoveniana* (2nd edition), Breitkopf & Härtel, Leipzig, 1925. See also under KASTNER, E.

Beethoveniana, J. Rieter-Biedermann, Leipzig, 1872.

Zweite Beethoveniana, published articles, with a foreword by E. Mandyczewski, J. Rieter-Biedermann, Leipzig, 1887. Second impression of *Beethoveniana* and *Zweite Beethoveniana*, C. F. Peters, Leipzig, 1925.

Beethoven's Studien, Vol. I, J. Rieter-Biedermann, Leipzig and Winterthur, 1873. No further volume issued.

PARRY, C. H. H.

'Variations', article in Grove's *Dictionary of Music and Musicians*, 5th edition, Macmillan, London, 1954.

PIERCE, E. H.

'The Significance of the "Trill", as found in Beethoven's most mature works', article in the *Musical Quarterly*, New York, Vol. XV, 1929.

PROD'HOMME, J.-G.

Les Sonates pour Piano de Beethoven, Delagrave, Paris, 1950. Original edition, 1911.

PROUT, E.

Fugue, 4th edition, Augener, London, n.d. (Preface dated December 1891).

RIEMANN, H.

'Beethoven und die Mannheimer', article in *Die Musik*, Berlin, Vol. VII, iii. 1908.

'Beethovens Prometheus-Musik ein Variationwerk', article in *Die Musik*, Berlin, Vol. IX, iii. 1910.

L. van Beethovens sämtliche Klaviersolosonaten, 3 vols., M. Hesse, Berlin, 1918, 1919.

SCHENKER, H.

Die letzten fünf Sonaten von Beethoven, critical edition with introduction and commentary (usually referred to as the *Erläuterungsausgabe*), Universal-Edition, Vienna, 1913 (Op. 109), 1914 (Op. 110), 1916 (Op. 111), 1921 (Op. 101).

SCHINDLER, A.

Biographie von Ludwig van Beethoven, 2 vols., Aschendorff, Münster, 1840. Reprint with commentary by Dr. A. C. Kalischer, Schuster & Löffler, Berlin and Leipzig, 1909.

SCHMID, E. F.

'Beethovens Bachkenntnis', article in *Neues Beethoven-Jahrbuch*, Brunswick, Vol. V, 1933.

SCOTT, M. M.

Beethoven (the 'Master Musicians' series), Dent, London, 1934. Fourth edition, Dent, London, 1943.

SEYFRIED, I. RITTER VON

Ludwig van Beethovens Studien im Generalbasse, Contrapuncte und in der Compositionslehre, T. Haslinger, Vienna, 1832.
Beethoven Études, a translation of the above by F. J. Fétis, M. Schlesinger, Paris, 1833.
Beethoven's Studies in thorough-bass, counterpoint and the art of scientific composition, a translation and edition of the original German by H. H. Pierson (Edgar Mansfeldt), Schuberth & Co., Leipzig, 1853.

SHEDLOCK, J. S.

'Gustav Nottebohm and the Beethoven Sketch-Books', two articles in the *Monthly Musical Record*, London, Vol. XIII, 1883.
'Beethoven's Sketch Books', various articles in the *Musical Times*, London, Vols. XXXIII–XXXV, 1892–4.
A Reference Catalogue of British and foreign Autographs and Manuscripts; Ludwig van Beethoven, Part VIII of a series edited by H. S. Wyndham, Society of Archivists, London, 1899.
Beethoven's Pianoforte Sonatas, Augener, London, 1918.

SONNECK, O. G. T.

Beethoven, Impressions of Contemporaries, collected by O. G. T. Sonneck, G. Schirmer, Inc., New York, 1926, and Oxford University Press, London, 1927.

SQUIRES, P. C.

'Beethoven's Concept of the "Whole" ', article in the *American Journal of Psychology*, Vol. 48, 1936.

SULLIVAN, J. W. N.

Beethoven: his Spiritual Development, Jonathan Cape, London, 1927.

THAYER, A. W.

Chronologisches Verzeichnis der Werke Ludwig van Beethovens, F. Schneider, Berlin, 1865.

Ludwig van Beethovens Leben, translated into German by H. Deiters, 5 vols.: Vol. I, F. Schneider, Berlin, 1866; Vols. II and III, W. Weber, Berlin, 1872, 1879; Vol. IV, completed by H. Riemann, with foreword, index, corrections, and supplements, and Vol. V, Breitkopf & Härtel, Leipzig, 1907, 1908; and subsequent editions.

The Life of Ludwig van Beethoven, an English edition of the above, revised and amended with the assistance of Thayer's original English manuscript by H. E. Krehbiel, 3 vols., The Beethoven Association, New York, 1921, 1922, 1925.

TOVEY, D. F.

A Companion to Beethoven's Pianoforte Sonatas, bar-to-bar analysis, The Associated Board of the Royal Schools of Music, London, 1931.

'Beethoven: Fifteen Variations and Fugue, "Prometheus", Op. 35', an essay in *Essays in Musical Analysis*, Vol. VI, Oxford University Press, London, 1939.

Beethoven, Oxford University Press, London, 1944.

TÜRK, D. G.

Kurze Anweisung zum Generalbassspielen, E. B. Schwickert, Leipzig, and Hemmerde und Schwetschke, Halle, 1791.

TURNER, W. J.

Beethoven: The Search for Reality, Benn, London, 1927.

VIEILLE, F.

État mental de Beethoven, Thesis, Lyons, Schneider, 1905.

WALKER, E.

'The Pianoforte Sonatas: some textual problems', article in the Beethoven Supplement to *Music & Letters*, London, Vol. VIII, 1927.

WEGELER, F. G., and RIES, F.

Biographische Notizen über Ludwig van Beethoven, K. Bädeker, Coblenz, 1838. Second edition, enlarged and with explanatory notes by Dr. A. C. Kalischer, Schuster & Löffler, Berlin, 1906.

Notices biographiques sur L. van Beethoven, a translation of the above into French by A. F. Legentil, Dentu, Paris, 1862.

WETZEL, H.

'Beethovens Sonate op. 110, eine Erläuterung ihres Baues', two articles in *Beethoven-Jahrbuch* (edited by T. Frimmel), G. Müller, Munich and Leipzig, Vol. II, 1909.

MANUSCRIPT

BEETHOVEN, L. VAN

Sketch-book, British Museum, Add. MS. 29801.

INDEX

INDEX